Grammar Rules!

Tanya Gibb

Australian Curriculum Edition

Name: ______________________________

Class: ______________________________

Grammar Rules! Student Book 2
Australian Curriculum Edition
ISBN: 978 0 6550 9250 6

Designer and typesetter: Trish Hayes
Illustrator: Stephen Michael King
Series editor: Marie James
Indigenous consultant: Al Fricker

Acknowledgement of Country
Matilda Education Australia acknowledges all Aboriginal and Torres Strait Islander Traditional Custodians of Country and recognises their continuing connection to land, sea, culture, and community. We pay our respects to Elders past and present.

This edition published in 2024 by **Matilda Education Australia**, an imprint of Meanwhile Education Pty
PO Box 118, Burwood, Victoria, Australia 3125
T: 1300 277 235
E: customersupport@matildaed.com.au
W: www.matildaeducation.com.au

First edition published in 2008 by Macmillan Science and Education Australia Pty Ltd

Publication data
Author: Tanya Gibb
Title: *Grammar Rules! Student Book 2*
Australian Curriculum Edition
ISBN: 978 0 6550 9250 6

A catalogue record for this book is available from the National Library of Australia

Printed in China by Central
Sep-23

Contents

NOTE TO TEACHERS AND PARENTS

Grammar Rules!

Grammar Rules! comprehensively addresses the interrelated strands of Language, Literature and Literacy in the **Australian Curriculum English V9**, 2022. The *Grammar Rules!* series supports students' development of knowledge, understanding and skills in reading, viewing, speaking, writing and creating texts.

The **Australian Curriculum English** recognises that learning in English is recursive and cumulative, so each book in the *Grammar Rules!* series is designed to build on concepts covered previously and for an expanding range of audiences and purposes.

Grammar Rules! provides a conceptually sound scope and sequence of context-based activities that support teaching and learning in English. Although the title for the series is *Grammar Rules!*, the series in not just about grammar. Each unit of work in the series begins at the level of the whole text by identifying purpose and audience for the model text, providing teaching opportunities to activate students' background knowledge of the topic or the text type, and then supporting students in reading comprehension. The texts provided can be used for discussion of text forms and features and sentence structures, as well as for vocabulary expansion. The texts can also be used as models for students to use when creating their own written, spoken or multimodal texts. The texts included in *Grammar Rules!* cover a variety of informative, imaginative and persuasive texts and hybrid texts that use elements of different types of texts.

Grammar Rules! also teaches the conventions of punctuation and some aspects of spelling (for example, plural nouns, suffixes, prefixes and compound words); literary elements such as onomatopoeia, rhyme and alliteration; and the way visual elements function to support or construct meaning. Other areas of the **Australian Curriculum English** covered in *Grammar Rules!* include critical reading and understanding character, setting and plot in narrative texts, as well as imagery in poetry.

Student Book 2

Units of work

Student Book 2 contains 35 weekly units of work presented in a conceptually sound scope and sequence. The intention is for students to work through the units in the sequence in which they are presented. See the **Scope and Sequence Chart** on pages 6–7 for more information. There are regular Revision Units that can be used for consolidation or assessment purposes.

The sample texts in *Student Book 2* are not tied to any particular content across other curriculum areas but are generally based on the theme of animals. This allows teachers and students to focus on the way language is structured in the different types of texts according to purpose and audience. Students can then use this knowledge to critically evaluate, respond to and create texts in other learning areas.

Icons

Encourages students to create texts of their own to demonstrate their understanding of the text structures and features taught in the unit. These activities focus on written language; however, many also provide opportunities for using spoken language to engage with others, make presentations and develop skills in using ICT.

Highlights useful grammatical rules and concepts. The rule is always introduced the first time students need it to complete an activity.

Tells students that a special hint is provided for an activity. It might be a tip about language features, or a reminder to look at a rule in a previous unit.

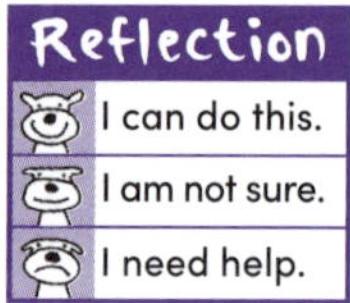

Encourages students to assess their progress across each unit.

Grammar Rules! Glossary

A valuable glossary is provided at the end of *Student Book 2*. Teachers and students can use this as a reference for terminology and rules introduced in *Student Book 2*. Page references are also given for the point in the book where the rule or tip was first introduced, so that students can go back to that unit if they need more information or further revision of the concept.

Grammar Rules! Student Book 2 (ISBN 9780655092506) © Tanya Gibb

Pull-Out Writing Log

At the centre of *Student Book 2* is a practical pull-out Writing Log so that students can keep track of the texts they have created or attempted to create. The Writing Log also includes a handy reminder of the writing process, as well as a checklist of types of texts for students to try.

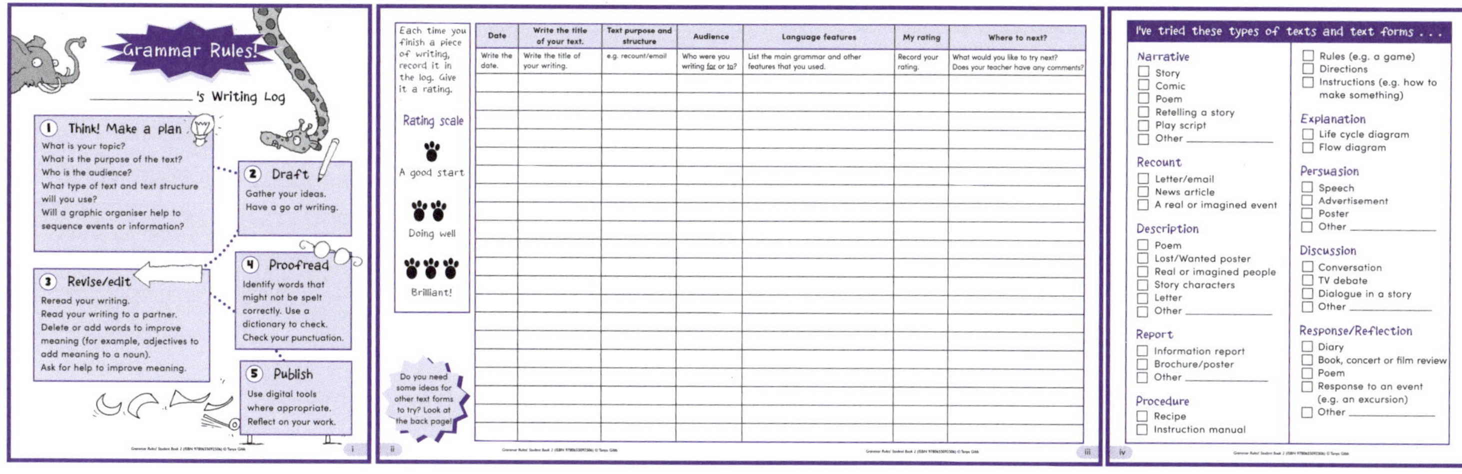

Unit At A Glance

Unit tag
States the main grammar focus

Type of text
Highlights the type of text and purpose of the sample text

Rule!
Introduces students to a new concept

Text sample
Provides a context for learning about language

Sequenced activities
Activities focus on reading comprehension, text features and structures, vocabulary or punctuation

Tip!
Reminds or gives a special hint

Try it yourself!
Gives students opportunities to apply their knowledge and skills to create their own texts. Students can engage in planning, drafting and editing their texts and using different modes and media to enhance presentation of their texts.

Reflection
Encourages students to assess their progress through each activity

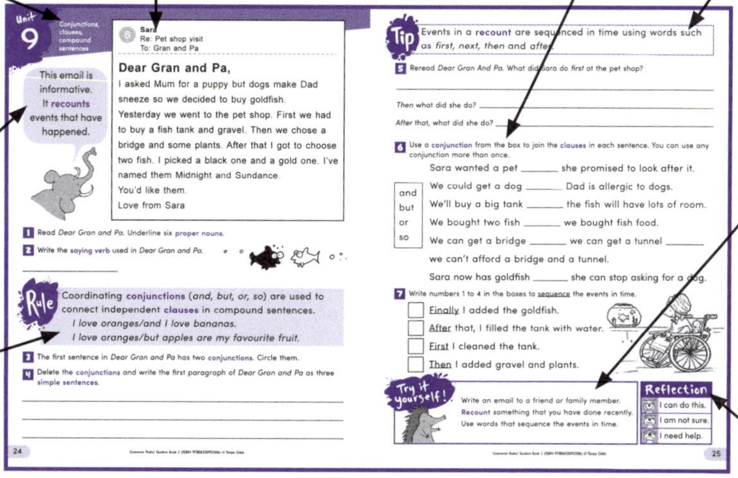

Grammar Rules! Teacher Resource Book 1–2

Full teacher support for *Student Book 2* is provided by *Grammar Rules! Teacher Resource Book 1–2*.

Here you will find valuable background information about teaching English along with practical resources, such as:

- strategies for teaching text structures and features
- literacy games and activities
- assessment strategies
- grammar and punctuation wall charts
- teaching tips for every unit in *Student Book 2*
- answers for every unit in *Student Book 2*.

SCOPE AND SEQUENCE

This scope and sequence chart is based on the requirements of the Australian Curriculum English.

Unit	Unit name Type of text	Purpose of text	Clauses, sentences, conjunctions	Nouns, noun groups, pronouns, adjectives	Verbs and verb groups	Adverbs, prepositional phrases	Elements of language
1	**Life Cycle of a Bird** Diagram	to inform		nouns	doing verbs		labels
2	**Bee** Diagram	to inform	clauses, simple sentences		being verbs		labels
3	**Move It!** Poem	to entertain	sentences, commas		doing verbs		commas in a series
4	**Sloths** Report	to inform	clauses, simple sentences	nouns	verbs		
5	**Uncle Waru** Response	to inform and share opinions	quoted speech		saying verbs		dialogue
6	REVISION						
7	**Children's Python** Recount	to inform	sentences	adjectives			opinions
8	**The Best Pet** Argument	to persuade		adjectives	thinking verbs		antonyms, opinions and reasons, dot points, paragraphs
9	**Dear Gran and Pa** Recount	to inform	coordinating conjunctions, compound sentences				sequencing events
10	**Where's My Mum?** Narrative	to entertain	conjunctions, sentences, compound sentences			prepositional phrases, adverbs	story map, animal characters
11	**Freddy and His Egg** Narrative	to entertain	exclamations			prepositional phrases	onomatopoeia, story characters
12	REVISION						
13	**How To Help Insects** Instructions	to inform/ instruct	commands	personal pronouns	verbs		
14	**Lost Dog** Map	to inform	directions, commands		doing verbs		compound words
15	**A Loony Cat** Description	to inform		personal pronouns			synonyms, main idea
16	**How** Poem	to entertain		singular and plural nouns		adverbs, prepositional phrases	
17	**Warrior** Response	to inform and share opinions		noun groups, adjectives			opinions and reasons
18	REVISION						

Grammar Rules! Student Book 2 (ISBN 9780655092506) © Tanya Gibb

Unit	Unit name Type of text	Purpose of text	Clauses, sentences, conjunctions	Nouns, noun groups, pronouns, adjectives	Verbs	Adverbs, prepositional phrases	Elements of language
19	**Giant Pandas** Response	to inform	conjunctions	noun groups, adjectives			opinions and reasons
20	**Wildlife Carer** Interview	to inform	questions and statements				fact and opinion
21	**Along Came a Spider** Narrative	to entertain	exclamations, quoted speech				
22	**How The Land Was Formed** Retelling	to inform	conjunctions	articles, noun groups	verbs		
23	**Llamas for Sale** Advertisement	to persuade	exclamations, questions				emotive and persuasive language
24	REVISION						
25	**Zoos** Discussion	to persuade		adjectives that compare			paragraphs, summarising
26	**How do Penguins Chicks Eat?** Explanation	to inform	questions	noun groups, pronouns, possessive adjectives		prepositional phrases	
27	**Reptile Encounter** Recount	to inform	sentences, conjunctions	noun groups			sequencing events and ideas
28	**Talk to the Animals Potion** Recipe	to entertain			doing verbs, being verbs		alliteration, rhyme
29	**Ringtail Possums** Report	to inform		adjectives	verbs	phrases	topic sentences, paragraphs
30	REVISION						
31	**Corroboree Frogs** Report	to inform	sentences	possessive pronouns	being verbs		
32	**The Chimp and the Crocodile** Narrative	to entertain	sentences		tense, verbs		summarising
33	**How to Help the Environment** Instructions	to inform	sentences	proper nouns	verbs, plural verbs, verb-subject agreement		
34	**How Sea Animals Breathe** Explanation	to inform	sentences, conjunctions		verbs		labels, summarising
35	REVISION						

Life Cycle of a Bird

The purpose of the diagram is to present information using drawings, labels and arrows.

1 Copy the simple sentences into the correct boxes on the diagram. These labels explain the life cycle of a bird.

The parent bird feeds the baby bird.
A chick grows inside the egg.
The mother bird lays an egg.
The young bird flies out of the nest.
The chick cracks out of the egg.
The parent birds build a nest.

Grammar Rules! Student Book 2 (ISBN 9780655092506) © Tanya Gibb

Nouns are words for people, places, animals and things, including ideas.

Common nouns: *mother beach bird nest happiness*

Proper nouns: *Emily Nunawading*
Glossy Black-Cockatoo Wollemi Pine

2 Write four **common nouns** used in *Life Cycle of a Bird*.

____

Verbs are words or word groups that tell what is happening in a clause. **Doing verbs** tell the actions.

is eating wriggles dangled swooped

3 Circle the **doing verb** in each set of words.

branch nest feathers chew

home swoop magpie noisy

hatchling parent gulp leaf

flutter beautiful beak pretty

4 Choose a **doing verb** from the box to complete each sentence.

dangled	opened	laid	grow	built

The mother bird ____________ three eggs.

The parents ____________ their nest on a high branch.

Chicks ____________ feathers.

The parent ____________ a worm for the chick.

The chick's mouth ____________.

Choose an animal. It might be one that lays eggs, such as a crocodile, a platypus or a dinosaur. Find out about the animal's life cycle. Draw a diagram with labels to explain each stage in the life cycle.

Reflection

 I can do this.

 I am not sure.

 I need help.

This **diagram** is informative. It has labels to show the parts of a bee.

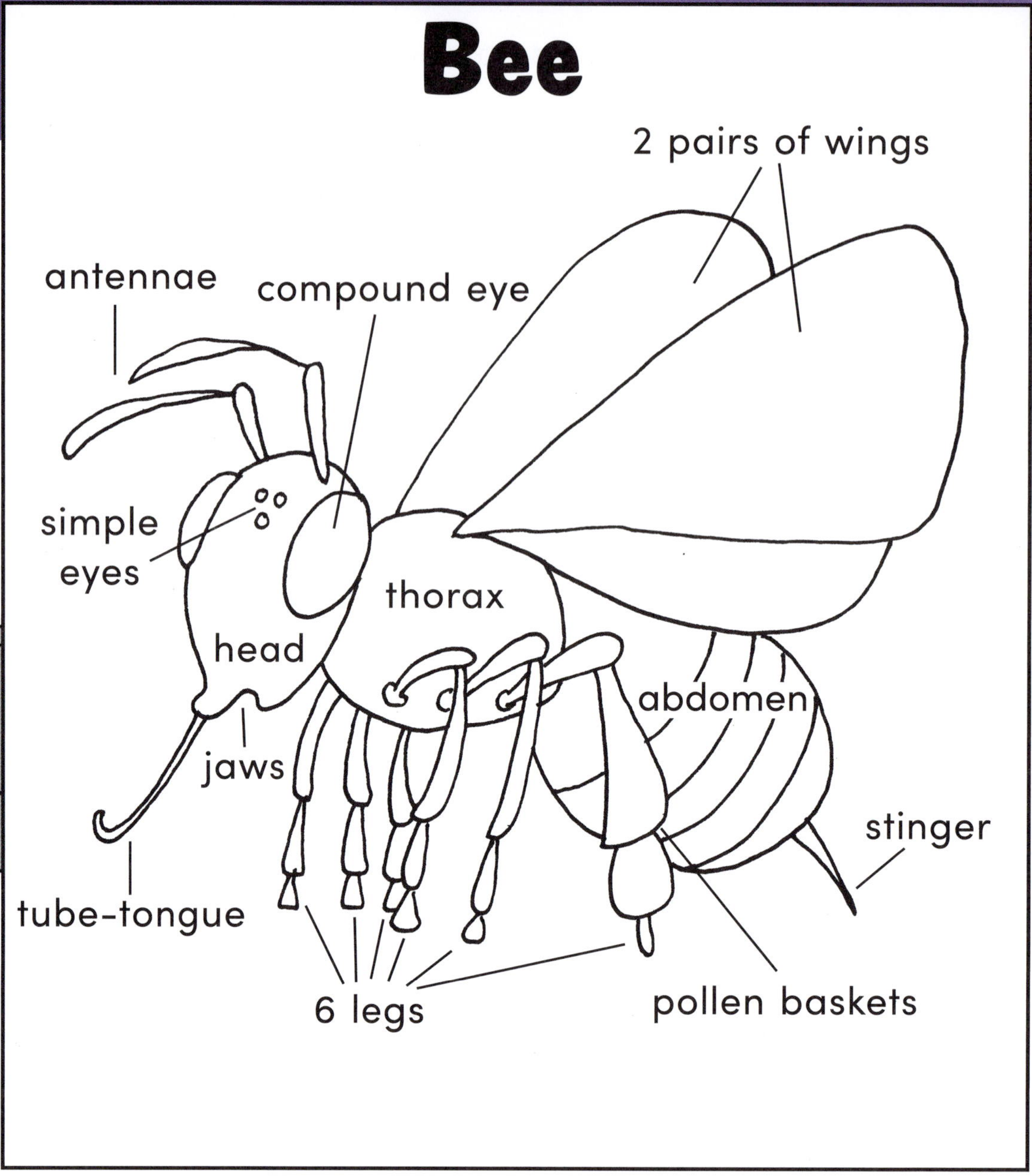

Bee

2 pairs of wings
antennae
compound eye
simple eyes
thorax
head
abdomen
jaws
stinger
tube-tongue
6 legs
pollen baskets

1 Look at the *Bee* diagram. Use a **common noun** to complete each sentence.

wings	legs	baskets	head	stinger

A bee's legs and ______________ are attached to its thorax.

Pollen ______________ are on the back legs.

The ______________ is on the end of the abdomen.

The antennae are on the bee's ______________.

Bees have six ______________.

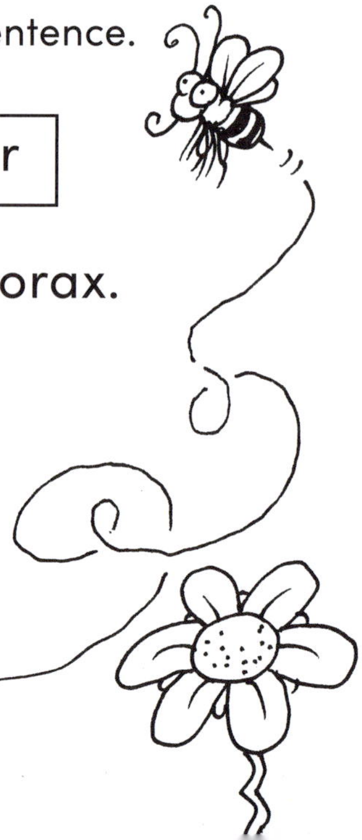

Grammar Rules! Student Book 2 (ISBN 9780655092506) © Tanya Gibb

Being (relating) verbs show what things are or what things have. You cannot see any action taking place.

is am are was were has have had

2 Use a **being verb** from the box to complete each sentence.

are
have
am
has
was

Bees ________ insects.

Bees ________ a stinger.

A bee ________ black stripes on an orange body.

I ________ six years of age.

Eric ________ careful not to step on the bee.

A **sentence** is a complete message. A sentence can be made up of one or more **clauses**. Every clause must have a **verb**. A simple sentence is one clause.

3 Write the words in the correct order to form **simple sentences**. Remember that a sentence begins with a **capital letter** and ends with a full stop, question mark or exclamation mark.

in their hives honey make bees

____

bees only female stingers have

____

good for sucking tube-tongues are nectar

____

Make up a crazy insect. Create a **diagram**. Label the body parts. Write three **sentences** to describe what it is or what it has. Use **being verbs**.

Reflection

 I can do this.

 I am not sure.

 I need help.

Unit 3

Doing verbs, sentences, commas

This poem lists the ways animals move. Its stanzas and sentences follow a regular pattern.

Move It!

Frogs leap,
hop, jump, swim.

Crocodiles run,
crawl, dive, roll.

Owls swoop,
fly, soar, glide.

Snakes slither,
slide, curl, sleep.

1 What is the poem about?

____

____

Rule **Commas** are used to separate parts of a sentence or words in a series.

Remember to buy apples, bananas, watermelon and pineapple.

2 Rewrite the sentences using punctuation markers to match the poem.

fleas crawl jump cling irritate

____

dolphins swim glide dive jump

____

3 Write four **common nouns** for other animals that swim.

__________ __________ __________ __________

4 Write four **common nouns** for other animals that jump.

__________ __________ __________ __________

5 Underline the **doing verbs** in *Move It!*

Grammar Rules! Student Book 2 (ISBN 9780655092506) © Tanya Gibb

6 Draw a line to match a **common noun** with a **doing verb**.

A horse	hovers.
A camel	gallops.
A monkey	prowls.
A shark	swings.
A fly	lopes.

7 Rewrite the sentence correctly.

allegra saw many cockatoos magpies butterflies and lizards on her walk

____

____

8 Write a **doing verb** to tell how each animal moves.

A worm ________________. A lion ________________.

An elephant ________________. A zebra ________________.

A flea ________________. A mouse ________________.

9 Circle the three **doing verbs** that describe your best moves.

running dancing jumping creeping skating hiding

tickling hopping throwing

10 Circle the **doing verbs** for what the wombat is doing.

claws digging burrowing swimming hole dirt mound tunnelling

Try it yourself!

Write a poem of your own using **doing verbs**. Read your poem to a group or the class. Use your voice to make your reading sound interesting.

This is an informative text. It is an **information report** about sloths.

Sloths

Sloths are mammals. They live in South America. Sloths have mostly brown fur. Sloths mainly eat leaves but sometimes they eat insects and lizards. Sloths are eaten by jaguars. Sloths sleep for at least fifteen hours every day. They spend a lot of time lying around in trees where they are hidden from view. When they are on the ground they walk very, very slowly. Sloths are probably the slowest animals on earth.

By Tsehay

1 Read *Sloths*. Write the **proper noun** for the place where sloths live.

____

2 Find a sentence in *Sloths* that includes a **being verb**.
Copy it onto the line.

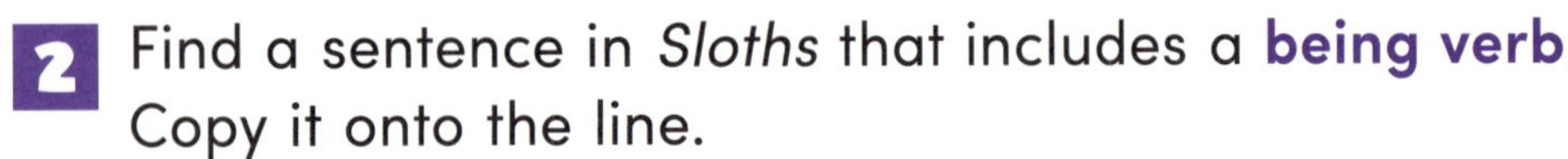

____

3 Underline three **doing verbs** in *Sloths* for actions sloths do.

The **subject** of a **clause** is the <u>who</u> or <u>what</u> that is doing the action.

<u>Sloths</u> sleep a lot. (Sloths are doing the sleeping.)

4 Use a **doing verb** from the box to complete each **clause**. Circle the subject of each clause.

sleep	eat	walk	hide	climb

Sloths ____________ leaves.

Sloths ____________ trees.

Sloths ____________ slowly.

Sloths ____________ from jaguars.

Sloths ____________ most of the day.

Grammar Rules! Student Book 2 (ISBN 9780655092506) © Tanya Gibb

5 Use a **common noun** from the box to complete each **simple sentence** with its subject.

Giraffes	Elephants	Koalas	Jaguars	Sloths

______________ eat sloths.

______________ reach into tall trees.

______________ swing their trunks.

______________ move slowly.

______________ eat gum leaves.

6 Circle the **being verbs** in these **sentences**.

Sloths are tree-dwelling mammals. They have mostly brown fur and are slow-moving, especially when they are on the ground.

7 Write the words in the correct order to form **simple sentences**. Use a **capital letter** to start each sentence. Use a **full stop** at the end.

on the branch the sloth sleeps

____

hugs a mother sloth its baby

____

the jaguar dinner hunts for

____

Choose an animal. Write an **information report** about the animal. Tell where it lives, what it looks like, what eats it and how it moves.

Unit 5

Saying verbs, quoted speech

This text is a response. The writer shares information and opinions.

Uncle Waru

Uncle Waru often visits our school. He tells us stories and shares his traditional knowledge. He sings to us in his language. He's a really good singer.

Uncle Waru is also helping us build a bush tucker garden. He says there are many native plants in Australia that we can eat. Some plants can be used as medicine, too.

I hope we can grow Kakadu plum (gubinge), lilly pilly, blue tongue berries and quandong.

By Phoebe

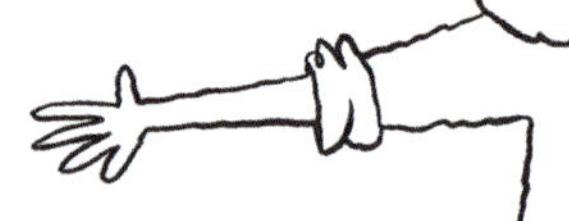

Rule **Saying verbs** are verbs that show you something is being said.

called *yelled* *whispered* *said*

1. Read *Uncle Waru.* Underline three **saying verbs**.

2. What does Uncle Waru do at the school?

____

____

3. Write the **proper nouns** in *Uncle Waru.*

____

4. How does Phoebe feel about Uncle Waru coming to the school? How do you know?

____

____

Grammar Rules! Student Book 2 (ISBN 9780655092506) © Tanya Gibb

Quoted speech is the actual speech someone says.
It can be written inside single or double **quotation marks**.

'Uncle Waru is here,' announced John.

5 Circle the words spoken by each person below.

'On Kalkadoon Country, Waru is a word for the Milky Way,' said Uncle Waru.

'Uncle Waru's country is near Mount Isa,' said Mr Leeton, our principal.

'That's right,' agreed Uncle Waru.

'Thank you for showing us so many things,' declared Molly.

6 Copy the series of items in *Uncle Waru* that Phoebe wants to grow. Use commas.

____

7 Work with a partner. Take turns saying the sentence below in the voice of each **saying verb** in the box.

warned	announced	shouted	gasped	sighed	giggled	sang
whispered	cried	laughed	scolded	sobbed	taunted	snorted

'You shouldn't be here,' ____________________ Matilda.

8 Write the words in the correct order to form a **statement**. Use correct punctuation.

is a native plum the Kakadu fruit

____

Work with a partner. Find a picture book or novel that includes a conversation in **quoted speech**. Read the conversation the way the **saying verbs** dictate.

Unit 6

Revision

1 Write the labels on the diagram. Put them in the correct order to explain the life cycle.

The larva then goes into its pupa stage.
An egg is laid.
The egg hatches into a larva.
The adult emerges.
The larva grows.

Life Cycle of a Beetle

1 ______________________

2 ______________________

3 ______________________

4 ______________________

5 ______________________

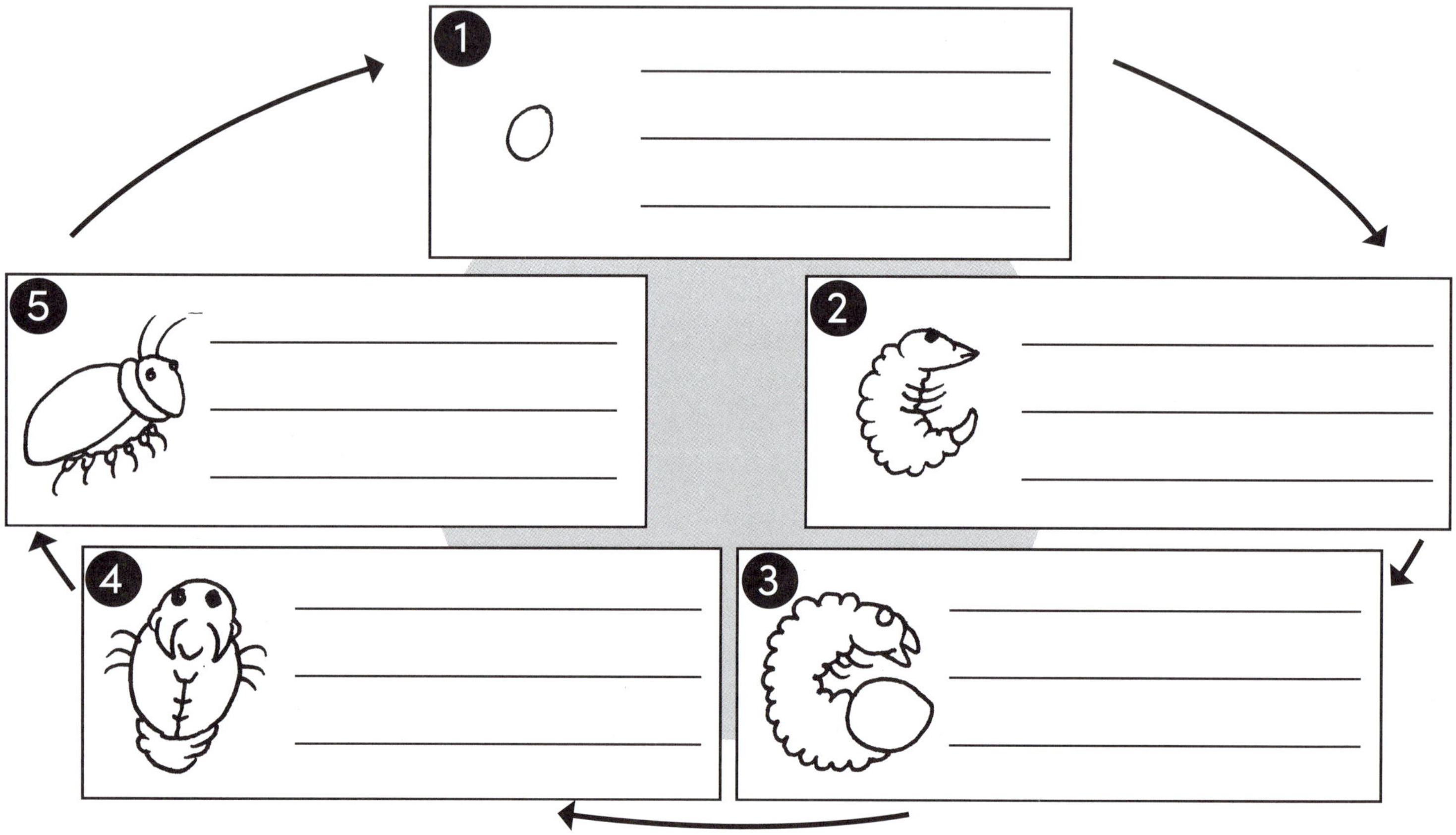

2 Write four **common nouns** from the Life Cycle of a Beetle.

____

3 Circle the **verb** in each sentence. Underline the **proper nouns**.

Louie's hamster ran away.

The mouse in Mr Augustine's pet shop had babies.

Possums live in the roof of Cate's house.

'Beetles have six legs,' stated Ms Holliday.

Grammar Rules! Student Book 2 (ISBN 9780655092506) © Tanya Gibb

4 Write a **saying verb** of your own on each line. Don't use *said*.

'I'm going to the zoo on Wednesday,' ________________ Dean.

'Will you take me with you?' ________________ Amira.

'I'll ask Mum,' ________________ Dean.

'Thanks. I'll keep my fingers crossed,' ________________ Amira.

5 Write a **doing verb** from the box in each **simple sentence**.

picked	buzzed	kicked	shared	climbed

A goat ________________ the mountain.

Flies ________________ around the cake.

Moana ________________ her banana.

Leila ________________ the ball.

Ollie ________________ strawberries.

6 Write the words in the correct order to form **sentences**. Use correct punctuation.

pond the croak in frogs

____

gubinge and grow quandong tomatoes we

____

like climb to goats mountains

____

7 Write a **being verb** on each line.

Bees ____________ insects. They ____________ six legs and two antennae.

Those broken glasses ____________ Zoe's. Luckily, she ____________ a spare pair.

The writer's purpose is to recount an experience and give an opinion about it.

Children's Python

My younger sister and I went to a talk at the zoo. It was interesting. The zookeeper showed us a Children's python. The species was named in 1842 after a man at a museum in England whose name was John George Children.

The python was beautiful. She was brown with darker brown splotches. Her skin felt smooth and was as soft as silk. When she was warm from being handled she became more active. Children's pythons can bite but she was very gentle and placid.

I enjoyed learning about the Children's python.

By Lottie

1 Read *Children's Python*. Underline four **common nouns**.

2 What is the writer's opinion about the talk at the zoo? Answer in a **sentence**.

---

3 What is the writer's opinion about the Children's python? Answer in a **sentence**.

Grammar Rules! Student Book 2 (ISBN 9780655092506) © Tanya Gibb

Adjectives build descriptions of **nouns**. Adjectives help the writer share an opinion and help readers form opinions.

cute kitten *timid dog* *sad monkey*

4 Find **adjectives** in *Children's Python* to describe these **common nouns**.

__________ sister __________ splotches __________ skin

__________ skin __________ snake __________ snake

5 Find three **adjectives** in *Children's Python* that tell you the writer has a positive opinion of the snake.

_______________ _______________ _______________

6 Describe the animals. Write an **adjective** from the box on each line.

heavy	tiny	tall	toothy	sleepy

__________ __________ __________ __________ __________

7 Finish the **sentence**.

The python's skin was as _______________ as __________________.

8 Circle the **adjectives** that might describe a dog you should NOT pat.

active greedy placid brown scary ferocious quiet soft

Try it yourself!

Write about an experience you have had. It could be about somewhere you have been or something you have done. Describe it and give your opinion about it.

Reflection

- I can do this.
- I am not sure.
- I need help.

Unit 8 Thinking verbs, antonyms

The writer's purpose is to present an opinion and persuade others to accept that opinion.

The Best Pet

I think mice are the best pets for these reasons:

- They are fun to watch when they run on their exercise wheel and play with their toys.
- They are really small so they are good pets if you live in a unit.
- They are simple to care for – just keep their home clean.
- Their food costs very little.

Those are the reasons why I believe mice are the best pets. If you want a pet, I recommend mice but get two so they can keep each other company.

By Kai

1 Read *The Best Pet*. Underline five **common nouns**.

2 What does Kai want people to believe? Write a **sentence** to answer.

____

3 The writer uses the **being verb** *are* in *The Best Pet*. Circle it.

How many times is it used? ☐

Thinking verbs are used for thoughts and feelings (*feel, think, hope, wonder*).

Sheng understands Kai's reasons. Meena believes Avi.

4 Complete each sentence with a **verb** from the box.

wants thinks feel want hope

I ____________ my pet mouse has babies.

I ____________ two mice.

Dad ____________ mice are fun to watch.

I ____________ very happy today.

Sheng ____________ pet mice, too.

Grammar Rules! Student Book 2 (ISBN 9780655092506) © Tanya Gibb

5 Write two **thinking verbs** used in *The Best Pet*.

6 Circle the **thinking verbs**.

worry agree wonder skip love jump

need concentrate like dislike cook understand

7 Write a **sentence** telling whether you agree or disagree with the writer of *The Best Pet* and why. Use **thinking verbs**.

8 Write a **sentence** that tells how you would feel about minding someone's pet mice for a few days.

Antonyms are words that mean opposite things.

hot → cold *reasonable → unreasonable*

9 Draw lines to link pairs of **antonyms**.

tall	smooth
thin	short
rough	quiet
loud	thick

10 Write an **antonym** for each **thinking verb**.

dishonest ____________

disagree ____________

disbelieve ____________

dislike ____________

Write a persuasive text about the animal you think is the best pet. Begin with a statement that gives your opinion. Then give your reasons. End with a summing up statement.

Reflection

I can do this.

I am not sure.

I need help.

Unit 9 Conjunctions, clauses, compound sentences

This email is informative. It **recounts** events that have happened.

Sara
Re: Pet shop visit
To: Gran and Pa

Dear Gran and Pa,

I asked Mum for a puppy but dogs make Dad sneeze so we decided to buy goldfish.

Yesterday we went to the pet shop. First we had to buy a fish tank and gravel. Then we chose a bridge and some plants. After that I got to choose two fish. I picked a black one and a gold one. I've named them Midnight and Sundance.

You'd like them.

Love from Sara

1 Read *Dear Gran and Pa*. Underline six **proper nouns**.

2 Write the **saying verb** used in *Dear Gran and Pa*.

____

Rule Coordinating **conjunctions** (*and, but, or, so*) are used to connect independent **clauses** in compound sentences.

I love oranges/and I love bananas.

I love oranges/but apples are my favourite fruit.

3 The first sentence in *Dear Gran and Pa* has two **conjunctions**. Circle them.

4 Delete the **conjunctions** and write the first paragraph of *Dear Gran and Pa* as three **simple sentences**.

____

____

____

Grammar Rules! Student Book 2 (ISBN 9780655092506) © Tanya Gibb

Tip Events in a **recount** are sequenced in time using words such as *first, next, then* and *after.*

5 Reread *Dear Gran And Pa.* What did Sara do *first* at the pet shop?

____

Then what did she do? ______________________________

After that, what did she do? __________________________

6 Use a **conjunction** from the box to join the **clauses** in each sentence. You can use any conjunction more than once.

and but or so

Sara wanted a pet ________ she promised to look after it.

We could get a dog ________ Dad is allergic to dogs.

We'll buy a big tank ________ the fish will have lots of room.

We bought two fish ________ we bought fish food.

We can get a bridge ________ we can get a tunnel ________ we can't afford a bridge and a tunnel.

Sara now has goldfish ________ she can stop asking for a dog.

7 Write numbers 1 to 4 in the boxes to sequence the events in time.

☐ Finally I added the goldfish.

☐ After that, I filled the tank with water.

☐ First I cleaned the tank.

☐ Then I added gravel and plants.

Write an email to a friend or family member. **Recount** something that you have done recently. Use words that sequence the events in time.

Reflection

 I can do this.

 I am not sure.

 I need help.

Unit 10 Prepositional phrases

This text is a **narrative**. It begins with the complication (problem) and ends when the problem is resolved. The animal characters speak.

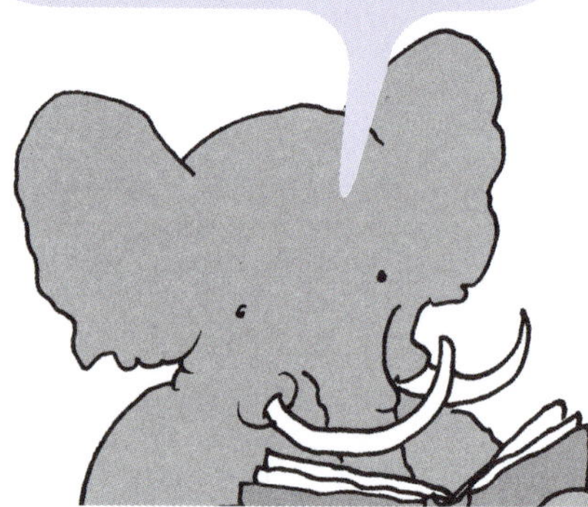

Where's My Mum?

The duckling woke from a nap and could not see his mother. He asked all the animals in the bush, 'Have you seen my mother?'

He asked:

the kangaroo under the tree,

the wombat in its burrow,

the possum below the branch,

the goanna beside the cave,

the kookaburra on the grass,

the bat in the cave,

the joey behind the tree,

and the platypus in the billabong

who said, 'There she is.'

1 Read *Where's My Mum?* Circle the **common nouns** for animals in the bush.

2 Mark the duckling's route around the bush. Use arrows. → → →

Grammar Rules! Student Book 2 (ISBN 9780655092506) © Tanya Gibb

Prepositional phrases can tell where, when or how.

on a giant rock *during the afternoon* *with its beak*

Adverbs also tell where, when or how.

here *there* *later* *soon* *quickly* *slowly*

3 Circle the **prepositional phrases** in *Where's My Mum?*

4 Add a word from the box to complete each **prepositional phrase**.

around toward through onto beside

The kangaroo jumped ____________ the duckling.

The joey waited ____________ the tree.

The possum peered ____________ the leaves.

The kookaburra fluttered ____________ the branch.

The duckling walked ____________ the bush.

5 Use a **conjunction** to join the **simple sentences**. Write each new **compound sentence**.

The wombat was thirsty. She didn't walk to the creek.

____

The platypus was curious. She came out of the water.

____

6 Use a **verb** from the box to complete each sentence. Circle the **prepositional phrases**.

raced flew hid

The tadpoles ____________ among the reeds.

The bats ____________ between the trees.

The emu ____________ across the grass.

Draw a map to illustrate a **narrative** that you have written. Include places on the map that your characters visit. Mark their route.

Reflection

- I can do this.
- I am not sure.
- I need help.

Unit 11

Exclamations, onomatopoeia, prepositional phrases

This text is the beginning of a **narrative**. It introduces the main character, his problem (the complication) and the setting.

Freddy and His Egg

Freddy was a baby dinosaur. His family lived on a beautiful mountain. Freddy never ventured beyond his beautiful mountain. His elders had warned him that terrifying creatures lived in The Beyond.

One morning Freddy woke in his nest to the sound of snapping branches. Snap! Crack! He looked up. It was a huge pterodactyl. The gigantic predator was standing over the nest trying to pick up an egg.

Freddy watched in horror as the egg rolled down the mountain and splashed into the dingy swamp far below, at the edge of The Beyond, with the pterodactyl swooping after it.

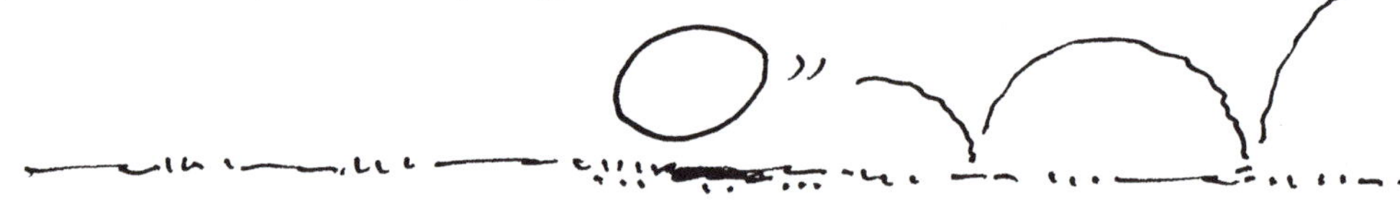

1 Circle two **exclamations** in *Freddy and His Egg*.

2 Write two **doing verbs** for what the egg did.

________________ ________________

3 Write a **prepositional phrase** for where Freddy lives.

____

Rule

An exclamation expresses strong emotion, surprise or a warning. It uses an exclamation mark. *Stop! Wow! I love it!*

4 How might Freddy feel about *The Beyond*? Answer in a sentence.

____

____

Onomatopoeia is the name given to words that sound like the thing they represent.

crash *clunk* *meow* *splat* *whizz*

5 Write two **onomatopoeia** words in *Freddy and His Egg*.

____________________ ____________________

6 Link each **onomatopoeia** word to the thing making the sound.

Splash!	the pterodactyl's beak at the egg
Thump!	the pterodactyl's wings in the air
Whoosh!	the pterodactyl's feet landing on the ground
Snap!	the egg falling into the water

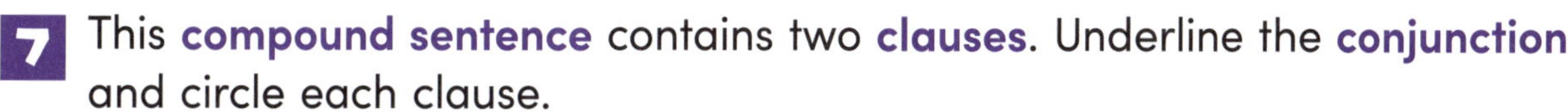

7 This **compound sentence** contains two **clauses**. Underline the **conjunction** and circle each clause.

The egg rolled down the mountain and it splashed into the dingy swamp.

8 Finish each sentence with a **prepositional phrase** of your own to tell where.

The egg sank ______________________________.

The pterodactyl flew ______________________________.

Freddy ran ______________________________.

Freddy's parents landed ______________________________.

Plant-eating dinosaurs lived ______________________________.

What will Freddy do? Write your own ending for *Freddy and His Egg*. Use **onomatopoeia** to make your story sound interesting. Remember to tell how your main character feels about events.

Unit 12 Revision

1 Write a **prepositional phrase** on the lines below each animal to tell where it lives or hides.

 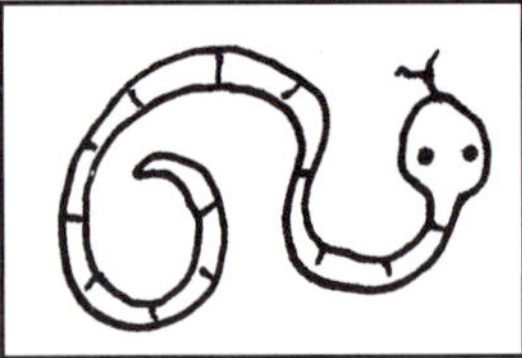   

______________ ______________ ______________ ______________ ______________

______________ ______________ ______________ ______________ ______________

2 Write a sentence for each **thinking verb** in the box.

thinks	feel	want	saw	imagine

____

____

____

____

____

3 Write an **antonym** for each word.

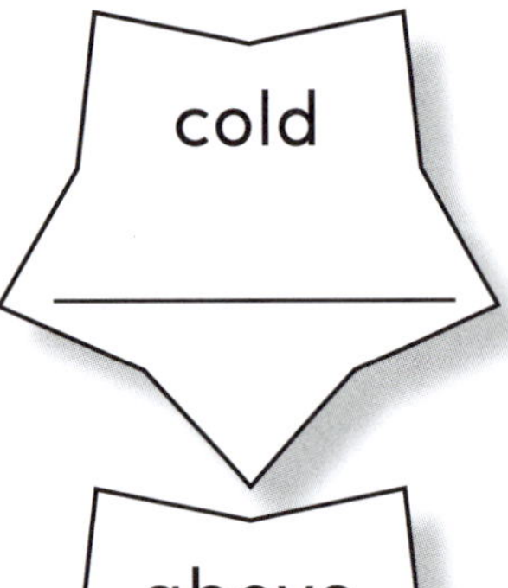

happy ______ cold ______ brave ______ light ______

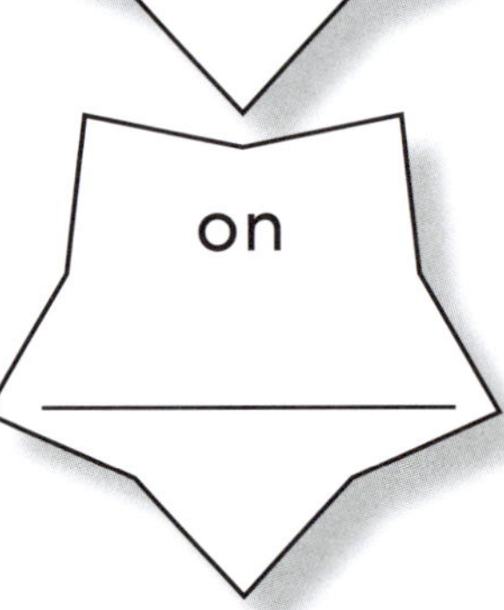

high ______ above ______ on ______ rough ______

Grammar Rules! Student Book 2 (ISBN 9780655092506) © Tanya Gibb

4 Use a **conjunction** from the box to join the clauses in each sentence.

or but and

I like vanilla ice cream __________ I eat ice cream every Sunday.

We can go to the movies __________ we can watch a movie on TV.

I could do better at cricket __________ I don't enjoy cricket practice.

5 Choose a word from the box to show the correct sequence of events.

Then First Finally After

__________ I set up the tank.

__________ I let the tarantula settle into the tank.

__________ that I put in some crickets.

__________ the tarantula ate the crickets.

6 Write a sentence for each **being verb** in the box.

is am are have had

____

____

____

____

____

7 Add an interesting **adjective** of your own to describe each **noun**.

the __________ dragon

two __________ black puppies

my __________ shoes

Sofia's __________ uncle

a __________ T-rex

a __________ bunch of grapes

a __________ holiday

an __________ story

a __________ bowl of freshly cooked noodles

Unit 13

Commands/ instructions, pronouns

The purpose of these **instructions** is to tell readers how to help insects.

How to Help Insects

We need insects to pollinate our plants and do other jobs for us. Insects need safe places to rest and to lay their eggs. You can help insects.

1. Avoid using pesticides.
2. Place small shallow plates of water with rocks in them in your garden so insects can land and have a drink.
3. Plant flowers, especially native flowers.
4. Leave a small corner of your garden in a natural state with bark and bare soil for ground-dwelling insects.

1 Why should you place a shallow plate of water in the garden?

____

2 Why should you avoid using pesticides?

____

3 Why should you leave bark on the ground?

____

4 Circle the **verb** that begins each instruction in *How to Help Insects.*

Commands are orders. They often begin with a **verb**.

Don't walk on the grass. *Do your homework.*

Instructions and directions are often written as commands. They tell what to do to achieve a goal.

Grammar Rules! Student Book 2 (ISBN 9780655092506) © Tanya Gibb

5 Use a **doing verb** from the box to begin each command.

Clean Feed Add Walk Pick

__________ the cat.

__________ the dog.

__________ the fish tank.

__________ up the dog's droppings.

__________ a bee hotel to the garden.

6 Write a **command** that a family member gives you. Use quoted speech with **quotation marks**.

____

Rule

A **personal pronoun** is a word that is used in place of a **noun**.

me I we us you he him she her it they them

I need that book. Will you pass it to me, please?

7 Underline three **personal pronouns** in *How to Help Insects*.

8 Use a **personal pronoun** from the box to replace the noun in brackets in each sentence. If the pronoun begins a sentence use a **capital letter** to start.

he them they him

(Harry) ________ is making a bee hotel. Give the bamboo to ________ (Harry).

(Marika and Georgie) ________ are going to the park. Would you like to go to the park with ________ (Marika and Georgie)?

Try it yourself!

Write a set of **instructions** to tell a reader how to do something. Have a classmate read your instructions to check that they are clear and easy to follow.

Reflection

I can do this.

I am not sure.

I need help.

This **map** is informative. It shows the location of things in the neighbourhood.

Lost Dog

Charlie's dog, Jet, has wandered away from home. Charlie has placed 'LOST DOG' posters all over the neighbourhood. Help Charlie find Jet.

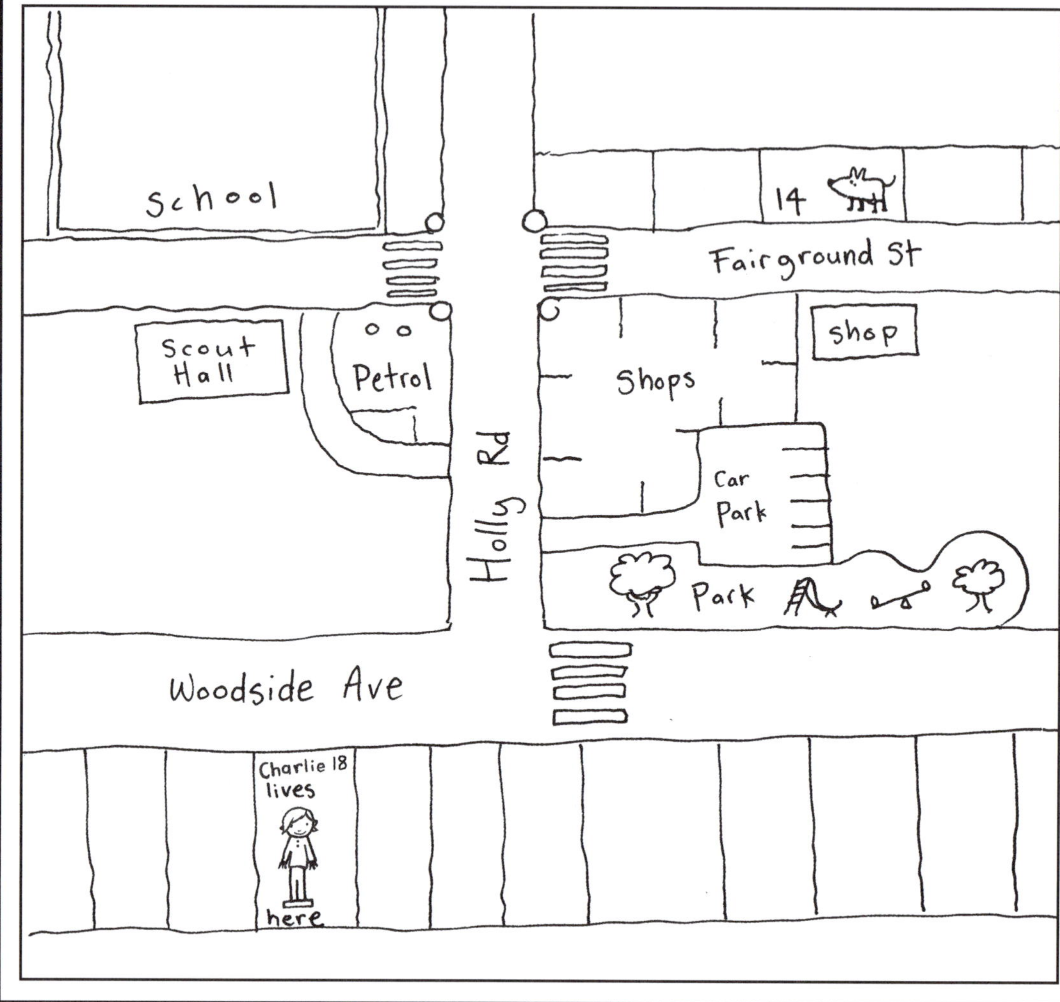

1 Look at the map. Look for Charlie. Look for Jet. Mark the route on the map with arrows and then write the directions below. Use **doing verbs** to start each **command**.

____

____

____

____

2 List three places Charlie will pass on the way to Jet.

____

Grammar Rules! Student Book 2 (ISBN 9780655092506) © Tanya Gibb

Compound words are words that are formed by combining two other words.

Sunday *blueberry* *classroom* *cardboard* *rainbow*

3 Draw a line to match the parts of the **compound words**.

back	noon
play	yard
ship	day
after	ground
birth	paper
news	wreck

4 Write a **compound word** for each illustration.

+ = ______________

 + = ______________

+ = ______________

+ = ______________

 + = ______________

5 Circle the **doing verbs** that you can do with a dog.

run mouth chase toes walk fetch teeth ears feet head roll tongue feed play tail tickle scratch pat nose wrestle lick leash

6 Write a **sentence** to describe a dog of your choice. Use **adjectives**.

____

____

7 What would Charlie have said to the person who found Jet?

____

____

Make a poster about Charlie's lost dog. Include **adjectives** to describe the dog. Write where it was last seen, its name, information about any reward and Charlie's contact phone number. Include a picture of the dog.

Reflection

I can do this.

I am not sure.

I need help.

Unit 15

Personal pronouns, synonyms, main idea

A Loony Cat

The writer's purpose is to describe their cat's behaviour.

Catnip is a herb. You can grow it in the garden. When you break open a catnip leaf you release a chemical that a large number of cats really love.

I have a cat that goes berserk when she smells catnip. She leaps and runs and pounces on the catnip leaf. She rolls on it and over it. She scratches it and paws at it. She licks it and then chews it, but then she spits it out. Then she growls and purrs and meows at it until she is exhausted. Then she has a catnap. She is really very funny to watch.

I think she deserves an award for craziest cat.

The **main idea** in a text is the idea that the writer or speaker wants you to believe or accept.

1 What is the **main idea** in *A Loony Cat*?

____

2 Write five **doing verbs** for things the cat does.

__________ __________ __________ __________ __________

3 Write the two **compound words** used in *A Loony Cat*.

__________ __________

Grammar Rules! Student Book 2 (ISBN 9780655092506) © Tanya Gibb

4 Circle all the **personal pronouns** in *A Loony Cat*. What **nouns** is *it* used for?

___

5 Write the **saying verbs** in *A Loony Cat*.

___ ___ ___

6 Which **personal pronoun** is used in place of the noun *cat*? ___

How many times is this **pronoun** used in *A Loony Cat*? ___

7 Add a **personal pronoun** to each line.

Lata and Matt have a new male cat. ___ have called ___ Leo. ___ got ___ from the RSPCA. Leo was an adult when they got ___ but ___ was only tiny. Lata says Leo is very happy living with ___ . ___ love Leo.

Rule

A **synonym** is a word that has a similar meaning to another word.

8 Write words from *A Loony Cat* that are **synonyms** for the words below.

adore ___

big ___

crazy ___

9 What does *berserk* mean? Use a dictionary.

___

Try it yourself!

Write a **description** of an animal's behaviour. Use **pronouns** so your text flows and is easy to follow. Read your description to your class.

Reflection

I can do this.

I am not sure.

I need help.

Unit 16

Singular and plural nouns, adverbs, phrases

This poem uses **adverbs** to tell how the animals move or behave.

How

Cats creep quietly
on soft pads.
Zebras run swiftly
with powerful legs.
Woodpeckers knock loudly
on the trunks of trees.
Penguin chicks sit warmly
on parents' feet.
Bear teeth rot easily
from too many sweets.
I sleep happily
in my cosy bed.

1 Read *How*. Underline the **doing verbs**.

Rule

A **singular noun** is for one thing. *toad*
A **plural noun** is for more than one thing. *toads*
A noun can be made **plural** by:

- adding *–s* or *–es* on the end *parent → parents*, *peach → peaches*
- changing *–y* to *i* to add *–es* *baby → babies*
- changing the spelling in another way *foot → feet*

Some nouns don't change at all from single to plural.
fish *sheep*

2 Write five **plural nouns** from *How* that end in *–s*.

____

3 Write a **plural noun** in *How* that does not end in *–s*. ______________

Grammar Rules! Student Book 2 (ISBN 9780655092506) © Tanya Gibb

Adverbs can modify verbs to tell how (*Cats creep quietly.*), **adjectives** (*Catnip is really special.*) and other **adverbs** (*Cats creep very quietly.*). Many adverbs end in *-ly*.

4 Circle six **adverbs** used in *How*.

5 Complete each extra **sentence** for the poem. Follow the same pattern as the poem.

Noun/pronoun	Verb	Adverb	Prepositional phrase
e.g. I	*sleep*	*happily*	*in my cosy bed.*
Dogs			
Dolphins			
Possums			
Snakes			

6 Use an **adverb** from the box to complete each sentence.

loudly
madly
widely
menacingly

The elephant trumpeted ________________.

The tiger prowled ________________.

The wolf howled ________________.

The hippo yawned ________________.

7 Write a **plural** for each **singular noun**.

horse ____________ elephant ____________ salmon ____________

fox ____________ mouse ____________ ostrich ____________

Write a poem. Use **adverbs** that tell how. Recite your poem to the class.

Reflection

 I can do this.

 I am not sure.

 I need help.

Unit 17

Adjectives, noun groups

The writer's purpose is to give an **opinion** about a painting. The opinion is supported with **reasons**.

Warrior

My favourite portrait at the art gallery is called *Moby Dickens*. It was painted by the artist Blak Douglas.

The painting shows a woman standing in an ocean of brown, sludgy-looking mud. Mud is everywhere, as far as the eye can see. The woman looks angry and fierce. She is staring straight out of the painting. She is carrying a bucket of muddy water in each hand but both buckets are leaking.

The grey sky is filled with dark, flat-bottomed storm clouds. It looks dangerous.

I really like this painting. I like that the woman looks strong and proud, like a warrior.

By Coral

1 Read *Warrior*. Complete the sentence below.

The subject of the painting is ______________________________

2 Circle the **being verbs** in *Warrior*.

3 Write the **prepositional phrase** used in *Warrior* to tell <u>where</u> the woman is standing.

____

4 Write five **adjectives** used in *Warrior*.

____

4 In paragraph 1, what does *It* refer to? ______________________________

5 In paragraph 3, what does *It* refer to? ______________________________

Grammar Rules!

____________________'s Writing Log

1 Think! Make a plan

What is your topic?
What is the purpose of the text?
Who is the audience?
What type of text and text structure will you use?
Will a graphic organiser help to sequence events or information?

2 Draft

Gather your ideas.
Have a go at writing.

3 Revise/edit

Reread your writing.
Read your writing to a partner.
Delete or add words to improve meaning (for example, adjectives to add meaning to a noun).
Ask for help to improve meaning.

4 Proofread

Identify words that might not be spelt correctly. Use a dictionary to check.
Check your punctuation.

5 Publish

Use digital tools where appropriate.
Reflect on your work.

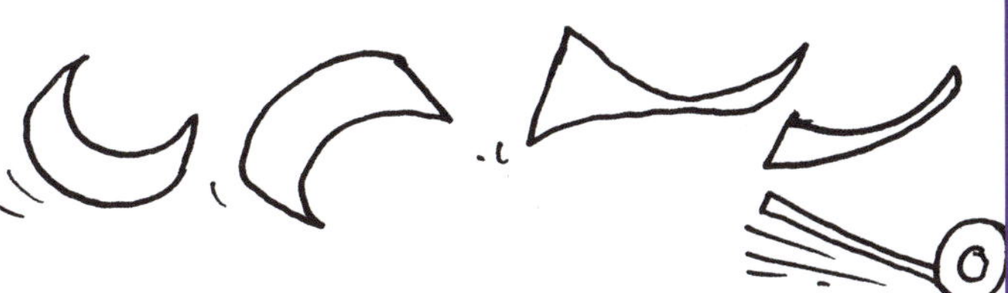

Each time you finish a piece of writing, record it in the log. Give it a rating.

Rating scale

A good start

Doing well

Brilliant!

Date	Write the title of your text.	Text purpose and structure	Audience
Write the date.	Write the title of your writing.	e.g. recount/email	Who were you writing <u>for</u> or <u>to</u>

Do you need some ideas for other text forms to try? Look at the back page!

Language features	My rating	Where to next?
ist the main grammar and other eatures that you used.	Record your rating.	What would you like to try next? Does your teacher have any comments?

I've tried these types of texts and text forms . . .

Narrative

- [ ] Story
- [ ] Comic
- [ ] Poem
- [ ] Retelling a story
- [ ] Play script
- [ ] Other ________________

Recount

- [ ] Letter/email
- [ ] News article
- [ ] A real or imagined event

Description

- [ ] Poem
- [ ] Lost/Wanted poster
- [ ] Real or imagined people
- [ ] Story characters
- [ ] Letter
- [ ] Other ________________

Report

- [ ] Information report
- [ ] Brochure/poster
- [ ] Other ________________

Procedure

- [ ] Recipe
- [ ] Instruction manual
- [ ] Rules (e.g. a game)
- [ ] Directions
- [ ] Instructions (e.g. how to make something)

Explanation

- [ ] Life cycle diagram
- [ ] Flow diagram

Persuasion

- [ ] Speech
- [ ] Advertisement
- [ ] Poster
- [ ] Other ________________

Discussion

- [ ] Conversation
- [ ] TV debate
- [ ] Dialogue in a story
- [ ] Other ________________

Response/Reflection

- [ ] Diary
- [ ] Book, concert or film review
- [ ] Poem
- [ ] Response to an event (e.g. an excursion)
- [ ] Other ________________

Grammar Rules! Student Book 2 (ISBN 9780655092506) © Tanya Gibb

A **noun group** is a group of words that includes a **noun**. A noun group can begin with an **article** (*a, an, the*) and include **adjectives** that describe (*an amazing painting*) or tell the number (*four magpies, some grapes*).

6 Circle the **noun groups**.

The grey sky has dark, flat-bottomed storm clouds floating across it.

Both buckets are leaking brown water.

A proud-looking woman is standing in brown, sludgy mud.

7 Write the correct **article** (*a, an, the, The*) on each line.

Zali saw ______ interesting artwork in ______ art gallery.

______ artwork was by Dr Treahna Hamm, ______ artist from ______ Wiradjuri and Yorta Yorta nations.

8 Underline the **adjectives** that tell quantity.

Bernie was first in line.

Frogs lay many eggs.

Three crocodiles swam past.

A few children are absent today.

9 Complete each sentence with **adjectives** from the box.

juicy grassy hungry sleek dirty oozy

The __________ dog rolled in the __________ mud.

The __________ horse galloped across the __________ paddock.

The __________ caterpillar ate the __________ leaf.

Try it yourself!

Write your **opinion** about an artwork you have seen or a book you have read. Say what you like or dislike about it. Use **adjectives** and **noun groups**.

Reflection

- I can do this.
- I am not sure.
- I need help.

Unit 18

Revision

1 Use a **doing verb** from the box to begin each **command**.

Buy	Run	Check	Mix	Take

__________ the letterbox.

__________ to the bus stop.

__________ a loaf of bread.

__________ this to the principal.

__________ the paint carefully.

2 Draw lines to match the parts of the **compound words**.

day	top
tooth	fall
door	light
water	brush
desk	bell

3 Write a **pronoun** on each line.

Cockatiels are a kind of parrot. __________ are smaller than cockatoos. Like a cockatoo, a cockatiel has a crest on its head, which __________ uses for communication. Cockatiels are about 30 cm tall. __________ have bright orange circles on their cheeks.

4 Use a **pronoun** to replace the **noun** in brackets.

He
She
It
They
them

(Mum) __________ is breeding frogs.

Give the worms to __________ (the fish).

(Tom) __________ loves Siamese fighting fish.

(The families) __________ are going to the school fete.

(The crocodile) __________ has sharp teeth.

Grammar Rules! Student Book 2 (ISBN 9780655092506) © Tanya Gibb

5 Use an **adverb** from the box to complete each sentence.

slowly cheekily bravely

Fifi ______________ hissed at the dog.

The turtle ______________ crawled away.

The monkey danced ______________.

6 Write a word from the box on each line to create **synonym** pairs.

tasty	chilly	gigantic	simple	little	horrible

awful ______________ cold ______________ easy ______________

huge ______________ delicious ______________ small ______________

7 Write a **plural** for each **singular** noun.

rabbit ______________ monkey ______________ walrus ______________

emu ______________ platypus ______________ echidna ______________

8 Underline the **noun groups**.

A funnel-web spider is hiding in there.

She caught the basketball.

He enjoys crossword puzzles.

9 Add one word from each box to each sentence to create **noun groups**. Use a **capital letter** if the adjective begins a sentence.

two	some	first	few

school	tomato	Siamese	football

Hossein ate ______________ ______________ sandwiches for lunch.

______________ dogs chased after the ______________ cat.

A ______________ fans watched the ______________ match.

The ______________ racer across the finish line was the ______________ student.

Unit 19

Noun groups, adjectives, conjunctions

The writer's purpose is to tell her class about her grandfather's trip.

Giant Pandas

My lucky grandpa went on a fabulous trip to China last month. He came back with photos of his visit with giant pandas in Chengdu. I really love his panda photos. The pandas look so soft and cuddly. They are huge. Grandpa said he had to wash his hands and wear a surgical gown and gloves, like a doctor, so that he didn't give the pandas germs. He fed carrots to one panda and held it in his lap while it ate. I would really love to go to Chengdu one day to see the pandas.

By Olivia

1 Read *Giant Pandas.* Underline the **proper nouns**.

2 Write three **describing adjectives** for what the pandas looked like.

________________ ________________ ________________

3 Circle the **pronoun** *he* in the text. Which **noun** does *he* replace? ________________

4 Find four words from the text that let readers know Olivia's opinion about things. They might be **adjectives** (*scary, loving, gorgeous, kind*) or **verbs** (*hate, avoid*).

________________ ________________

________________ ________________

5 If Olivia had a conversation with a friend, what might she say about Grandpa's trip? Use **quoted speech**.

____

____

Grammar Rules! Student Book 2 (ISBN 9780655092506) © Tanya Gibb

6 Circle the **noun groups**.

I saw six fat piglets.

Emily looked at the three tiny kittens.

We ate five delicious freshly baked cookies.

Arthur collected 25 cans for recycling.

Tip Remember the rule about **noun groups** on page 41.

7 Add an **adjective** from the box to complete each **noun group**.

muddy old five new happy

Billy owns __________ goldfish.

Gran collects __________ stamps.

The dog had __________ feet.

They have photos of a __________ holiday.

We are moving to a __________ house.

8 Use a **conjunction** (*or, so, but, and*) to join the **clauses** on each line.

Pandas like to eat bamboo __________ they also like carrots.

Grandpa wore gloves __________ he would not give the pandas germs.

Olivia's mother hopes to go to China __________ Olivia's stepfather does not want to go to China.

Grandpa might go to New Zealand next, __________ he could go to Fiji.

Write how you feel about something that is special to you. Describe its features using **noun groups**. Share your text with a partner.

Unit 20 Questions and statements

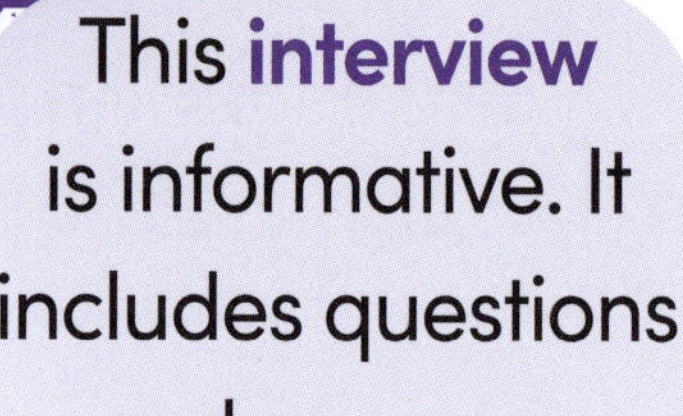

Wildlife Carer

A wildlife carer visited our school. These are some questions we asked, and her answers.

What kinds of animals do you look after?

I look after any sick, injured or orphaned native animals. I often care for native birds and possums.

How do you know what to do for the animals?

I had training. Plus there is a buddy system. When you first become an animal carer you are matched with someone with more experience than you. My buddy helped me a lot.

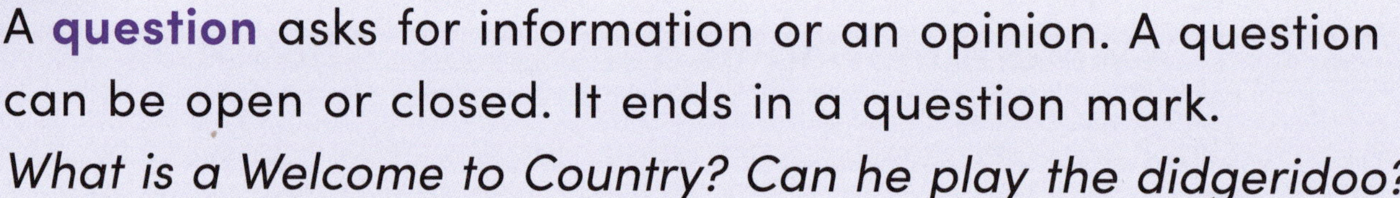

Rule A **question** asks for information or an opinion. A question can be open or closed. It ends in a question mark.
What is a Welcome to Country? Can he play the didgeridoo?

1. Read *Wildlife Carer.* Underline the two **questions**.
2. An **open question** requires a detailed answer. Write three open questions to ask the wildlife carer.

____

____

____

Rule A **statement** can be a **fact**. *Polar bears live at the North Pole.*
A **statement** can give an **opinion**. *Polar bear cubs are cute.*
Statements end in a full stop.

3. Answer the **question** with a **statement** that gives your **opinion**.
Would you like to be a wildlife carer? Why or why not?

____

____

Grammar Rules! Student Book 2 (ISBN 9780655092506) © Tanya Gibb

4 Write the possum's answer.

5 Write the pelican's answer.

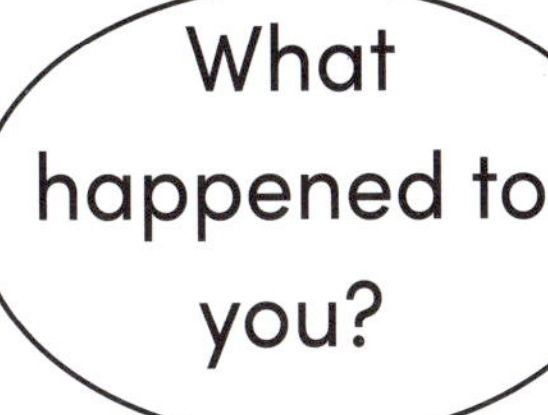

6 Tick a column to show whether each **statement** gives a **fact** or an **opinion**.

	Fact	Opinion
Dogs have four legs.	______	______
Lucy is scared of dogs.	______	______
Wombats are mammals.	______	______
I love wombats.	______	______

7 Write a **fact** about the spider picture.

____

Write an **opinion** about the spider picture.

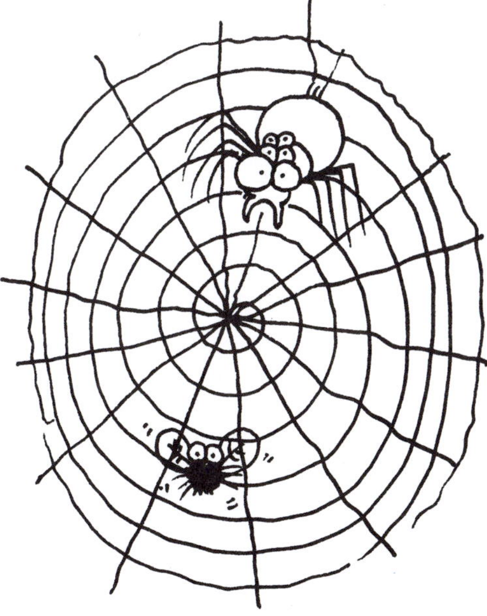

____

Work with a partner. **Interview** a student or teacher at your school. Ask them three **open questions** about their favourite animal. Write the **questions** and their answers.

Reflection

 I can do this.

 I am not sure.

 I need help.

Unit 21

Exclamations, quoted speech

Along Came a Spider

Once upon a time Millie Muffet was sitting in her bedroom listening to music when all of sudden a spider dropped from the ceiling next to her. Millie Muffet jumped up off her chair.

'Oh!' she cried. 'You poor little thing! Did you hurt yourself? You don't belong in here. Let me help you.'

Millie Muffet kindly took the spider in her hands and set it free out the back door.

This narrative is a modern version of the nursery rhyme *Little Miss Muffet.*

1 Read *Along Came a Spider.* Write the words used that often begin a nursery rhyme.

____

2 Where must Millie think the spider belongs? ______________________________

3 Underline the **quoted speech** in *Along Came a Spider.*

4 Write two **adjectives** that could describe the spider. ______________ ______________

5 Write four **adjectives** of your own to describe Millie's behaviour.

______________ ______________ ______________ ______________

6 Write the **pronouns** that refer to Millie Muffet in *Along Came a Spider.*

______________ ______________

7 Write the **question** from *Along Came a Spider.*

____

Grammar Rules! Student Book 2 (ISBN 9780655092506) © Tanya Gibb

8 How can you tell that *Along Came a Spider* is set in modern times?

____

9 Circle the **exclamations** in *Along Came a Spider.*

10 Write an **exclamation** for what you would say if you saw the spider.

____

11 Write an **exclamation** in **quoted speech** for each situation.

Marty breaks a glass. ______________________

Prisha gets a great birthday gift. ______________________

Zac thought a First Nations dance performance was deadly.

____

Natalia is about to step on broken glass but Riku warns her.

____

12 Rewrite each **sentence** correctly. Remember the punctuation marks.

i'll clean up after ziggy said sam

____

are you going to do it now asked eddie

____

do it now commanded mum

____

Choose a nursery rhyme such as *Little Bo Peep Has Lost Her Sheep* or *Jack and Jill Went Up the Hill.* Write a modern-day **narrative** version to perform with classmates.

Unit **22** Articles, noun groups, verbs, conjunctions

This text is informative. It tells about a Gundungurra Dreaming story that explains how the land was formed.

How The Land was Formed

The area around the Blue Mountains is on Gundungurra Country. The land was carved out when two giant ancestral spirits had a big battle. One was the giant Gurangatch, part-snake and part-fish. The other was the giant Mirrangan, a quoll.

Their battle began when Mirrangan tried to catch Gurangatch to eat. Gurangatch escaped, burrowing into the earth and carving out great caves, tunnels and rivers. Mirrangan ran above the ground, digging deep holes to try to reach Gurangatch underground.

Gurangatch managed to escape but is still hiding in the waters on Gundungurra Country.

1 Read *How the Land was Formed.* What landforms did the two giant ancestor spirits make?

______________ ______________ ______________

2 What kind of animal was Mirrangan? ______________

3 What kind of animal was Gurangatch? ______________

4 Where does Gurangatch live? ______________

5 Underline the **proper nouns** in *How the Land was Formed.*

6 Complete these **noun groups** from *How the Land was Formed.*

two ______________ ______________ spirits ______________ tunnels

______________ holes ______________ caves a ______________ battle

Grammar Rules! Student Book 2 (ISBN 9780655092506) © Tanya Gibb

7 Write **doing verbs** from the box to complete the sentences.

dug	burrowed	carved	chased

Gurangatch ____________ underground through the earth.

Gurangatch ____________ out great caves, tunnels and rivers.

Mirrangan ____________ Gurangatch.

Mirrangan ____________ deep holes.

8 Write the correct **article** (*a, an, the*) on each line. If the article starts a sentence, it needs a **capital letter**.

______ quoll is a small, meat-eating marsupial.

Quolls are under threat in ______ wild.

______ Eastern Quoll is now extinct on mainland Australia.

9 Use a **conjunction** from the box to join the **clauses** in each sentence.

and	so	but	or

Mirrangan had to escape ______ he would have been eaten.

Gurangatch carved out tunnels ______ Mirrangan dug big holes.

Gurangatch loves the water ______ Mirrangan does not like to swim.

The story of Mirrangan and Gurangatch is told ______ that people know how the land was formed.

10 Circle the **compound word** in *How the Land was Formed*.

Find and read an Australian First Nations Dreaming story. Retell it in your own words to a friend or a class group. Use volume, pace and emphasis to engage your audience.

Unit **23** Emotive and persuasive language

Llamas for Sale

Beautiful brown eyes, long eyelashes, gentle and friendly.

How can you resist?

Llamas **NEEDING GOOD HOMES**

Today only! Three Llamas for $300.

All they need now is a good owner and a large paddock.

Also – for a limited time only – three bales of hay, as well as a llama brush, free with all sales.

So, what are you waiting for?

This fabulous offer is for today only **so don't miss out!**

(NB: Llamas not sold separately.)

1 Read *Llamas for Sale*. Write the **noun group** that describes the llamas' eyes.

____

2 Write a **noun group** that could describe a suitable home for a llama.

____

3 Write two **questions** from the text.

____

4 Write the **exclamation** from the text that is a compound sentence.

____

____

Grammar Rules! Student Book 2 (ISBN 9780655092506) © Tanya Gibb

5 Why might the llamas need new homes? Write three possible reasons.

____

____

____

Rule

Emotive words are used to make you think or feel a certain way about a topic.

Don't miss out! *helpless kittens* *proud warrior*

6 Underline the **emotive words** in *Llamas for Sale*. These are all the words that might be used in the advertisement to persuade you to buy the llamas.

7 *Llamas for Sale* uses the **emotive words** *Don't miss out*. How do you feel when you miss out on something that you really want?

____

____

8 Tick the sentence in each pair that is most persuasive.

☐	You will love these.	☐	You might like these.
☐	You must get one.	☐	Maybe get one.
☐	It's a little bit friendly.	☐	It's very friendly and lovable.
☐	Offer only on today.	☐	No offers available.
☐	Lazy and stubborn.	☐	Intelligent and easy to train.

9 Complete the sentence.

Llamas are lovable because ______________________________.

Try it yourself!

Write an **advertisement** for a pet. It can be a real pet or a pretend pet. Write the pet's breed. Describe what it looks like. Describe its habits. Use **emotive words** that will persuade someone to buy it.

Reflection

- I can do this.
- I am not sure.
- I need help.

Unit 24 Revision

1 Write a sentence for each **personal pronoun** in the box.

he
she
it
they
I

____

____

____

____

____

2 Underline the **noun groups**.

The llama has lovely brown eyes.

The friendly llamas stood together.

Llama farms produce llama wool.

The scarf was made of soft llama wool.

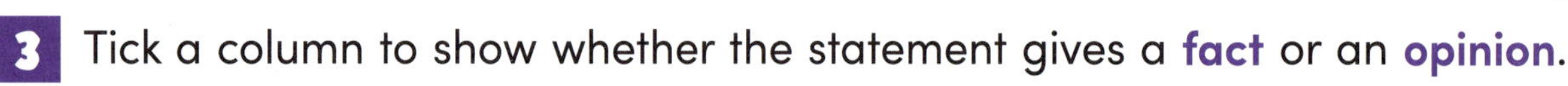

3 Tick a column to show whether the statement gives a **fact** or an **opinion**.

	Fact	Opinion
Llamas have ears.	______	______
Llamas are beautiful.	______	______
Echidnas are friendly.	______	______
Female kangaroos have pouches.	______	______
Wombats dig.	______	______

4 Answer the **question** with your **opinion** and **reasons**.
Would you like to live on a farm?

____

____

Grammar Rules! Student Book 2 (ISBN 9780655092506) © Tanya Gibb

5 Imagine you are going to buy three llamas. Write two **open questions** to ask the person selling the llamas.

____

____

6 Add an **adverb** of your own to each sentence to tell how.

The spider ______________ spun its web.

A mob of kangaroos bounced ______________ across the field.

Kookaburras laughed ______________ from the treetops.

The koala slept ______________ in the fork of the tree.

7 Rewrite each sentence with correct punctuation.

heidi grows tomatoes quandong gubinge and strawberries

____

do you like strawberries asked clay

____

8 Add a **conjunction** to each sentence.

Tasha likes llamas ____________ Nico does not like llamas at all.

Tasha likes llamas ____________ Lev likes llamas, too.

Gisele likes llamas ____________ she lives on a farm ____________ she can buy some llamas.

9 Tick the most persuasive sentence in each line.

☐	I think you'll want one.	☐	I know you'll want one.
☐	You must have one.	☐	Maybe you should get one.
☐	It's quite cute.	☐	It's absolutely gorgeous.

Unit 25

Paragraphs, adjectives that compare, summarising

The writer's purpose is to present different opinions about zoos.

Zoos

Zoos are popular places to visit but is it 'right' to keep wild animals in cages?

Some people believe that zoos are cruel. These people think that animals should live in their natural habitat in the wild.

Other people say that zoos do an important job. Zoos study animals to learn more about helping them survive. Zoos also try to breed endangered animals. Then, if they do disappear from the wild, at least they can survive in zoos.

I think zoos do a good job of teaching people about animals. I think zoos are necessary.

Rule A **paragraph** is a sentence or a number of sentences based on the same idea. A paragraph begins on a new line.

1 Read *Zoos*. Summarise the main idea of each **paragraph**.

Paragraph 1: Introduction	Paragraph 2: One point of view
______________________ ______________________ ______________________	______________________ ______________________ ______________________
Paragraph 3: Different point of view	**Paragraph 4: Summing up**
______________________ ______________________ ______________________	______________________ ______________________ ______________________

Grammar Rules! Student Book 2 (ISBN 9780655092506) © Tanya Gibb

Adjectives can be used to compare things. *hot hotter hottest*
Adjectives with more than two syllables use more or most to compare. *beautiful more beautiful most beautiful*

2 Add an **adjective** from the box to complete each sentence.

funny funnier funniest

Kathryn said, 'Monkeys are _______________.'

'Chimpanzees are the _______________ of all apes,' said Mohammed.

Eliza commented, 'Orangutans are _______________ than monkeys.'

'This is the _______________ book I've ever read,' declared Blake.

'I like _______________ books too,' said Carlos.

3 Write two **thinking verbs** used in *Zoos*.

____

4 Write five **adjectives** from *Zoos*.

____

5 Write three **prepositional phrases** that tell where used in *Zoos*.

____

6 What does the writer of *Zoos* think about zoos?

____

What do people at your school think about zoos? Interview adults and students. Write a **discussion** to present the points of view. Write in paragraphs.

Unit 26 Noun groups, personal pronouns

This **explanation** is informative. Its purpose is to explain how penguin chicks eat.

How Do Penguin Chicks Eat?

Many birds regurgitate food for their chicks to eat. This is a bit like vomiting.

There are three ways that penguin chicks can be fed. It depends on what species they are.

1. The parent swallows the fish. It travels to the penguin's stomach. Here, a special chemical stops the fish from being digested. A few days later the parent regurgitates the fish for the chick. The fish is as fresh as ever.
2. The parents partly digest their fishy food. Then they regurgitate slop into their chick's mouth.
3. The parent totally digests the fish. The fish then turns into very rich oil. The parent feeds this to the chick.

Do you have a pet bird? Has it ever regurgitated some of its food onto you? That means it loves you very much.

Rule Words in a **noun group** can:

- point out *that penguin chick*
  these those that
- show ownership *their baby*
  his her their your my our its

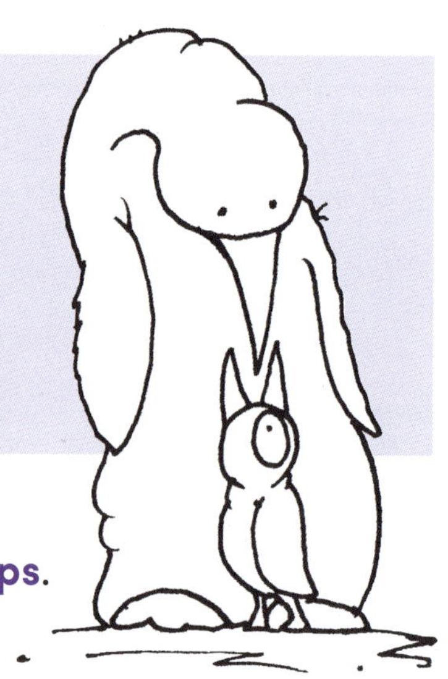

1 Read *How Do Penguin Chicks Eat?* Underline any four **noun groups**.

2 Underline the **noun group** in each sentence.

We won't eat these squishy old bananas. My little puppy watched us.

Those monkeys are sleeping. That monkey is cheekiest.

Grammar Rules! Student Book 2 (ISBN 9780655092506) © Tanya Gibb

3 Draw a diagram with arrows to show the sequence in step 1 of *How Do Penguin Chicks Eat?* Label each box.

4 Add a **prepositional phrase** from the box to complete each simple sentence.

with scaly skin	on blood	from a flower
into the chick's mouth	on its underside	

The parent penguin regurgitates food ________________________.

An octopus's mouth is ________________________.

A vampire bat feeds ________________________.

A hummingbird sucks nectar ________________________.

A reptile is a cold-blooded animal ________________________.

5 Circle the **personal pronoun** *It* in step 1 of *How Do Penguin Chicks Eat?* What **noun group** does *It* replace?

____

6 Circle the **personal pronoun** *it* in the last paragraph of *How Do Penguin Chicks Eat?* What **noun group** does *it* replace?

____

7 Finish the sentence.

Regurgitating is a bit like ________________________.

Try it yourself!

Write an **explanation**. You might choose to explain why bats hang upside down or why a cow's stomach has four sections. Write your explanation in a logical sequence.

Reflection

- I can do this.
- I am not sure.
- I need help.

Unit 27

Noun groups, sentences, conjunctions

The writer's purpose is to inform readers about events that have happened and give an opinion.

Reptile Encounter

Last Monday my class went on an excursion to see reptiles.

Firstly, we saw an eastern blue-tongue. It mainly eats snails. It felt very smooth. Then we saw a shingleback. It has a short round tail, which predators think is its head. It's rough and bumpy-looking. Flowers are its favourite food. After that we saw crocodiles and snakes. Lastly, we saw a number of different kinds of geckoes. They can all be found in Australia.

I learned a lot about reptiles on that excursion.

1 Read *Reptile Encounter*. Underline the **noun groups** that name four kinds of reptiles.

2 What is the job of the first **paragraph** in *Reptile Encounter*?

____

3 List the events described in *Reptile Encounter*.

Firstly, ________________________________

Then ________________________________

After that ________________________________

Lastly, ________________________________

4 What is the job of the last **paragraph** in *Reptile Encounter*?

____

5 Circle the **personal pronoun** *They* in *Reptile Encounter*.
Write the **noun group** that *They* represents.

____

Grammar Rules! Student Book 2 (ISBN 9780655092506) © Tanya Gibb

Extend **noun groups** to build descriptions. Descriptions can be positive or negative.

Mika saw a bumpy-looking shingleback with a short, round tail.

Zane saw a terrifying alien with yellow eyes.

6 Build your own descriptions. You can use a dictionary or the internet for ideas.

Noun	Noun group with adjectives
a shingleback	a flower-eating shingleback
a crocodile	
the snake	
a lizard	
the turtle	
the dinosaur	

7 Add **conjunctions** to link the **simple sentences**. Write the new sentences.

We like to watch the turtles. We prefer to watch the crocodiles.

____

Freya loves blue-tongue lizards. She also loves tortoises.

____

Freya loves blue-tongues. She visited the blue-tongues first.

____

Draw a **map** of the reptile park in *Reptile Encounter*. Add any other reptiles you choose. Use arrows to mark a route around the park for the **sequence** described in *Reptile Encounter*. Then mark the route you would take.

Reflection

- I can do this.
- I am not sure.
- I need help.

Unit 28

Alliteration, rhyme, verbs

This recipe for a magic potion is imaginative. Its purpose is to entertain.

Talk to the Animals Potion

WARNING! THIS MAGIC POTION IS VERY DANGEROUS.

Only use a little bit.

Ingredients

1 empty snail shell

4 flamingo feathers

11 leaves off a lemon tree

5 pink petunia petals

3 thimbles of thistledown

6 cups cow cream

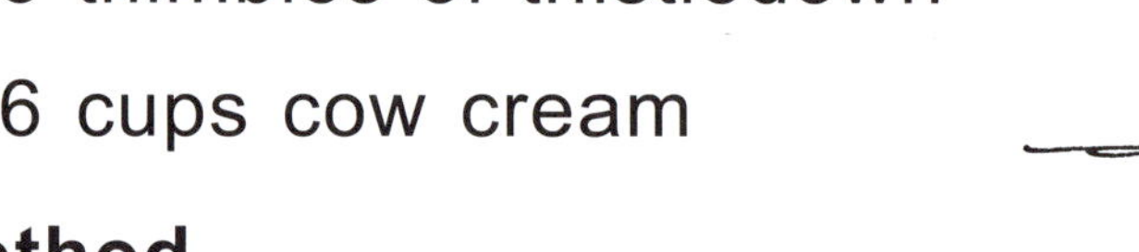

Method

1. Grind shell, feathers, leaves and petals.
2. Mix all ingredients together.
3. Apply to skin. Leave on for 24 hours.
4. Dance the cha-cha and chant three times: 'Animal lingo ling-gwistic ling-gwini la la.'
5. Rinse the potion off in the ocean.

WARNING: If animal voices sound weird, you need to use the magic <u>remedy</u>.

1 Work with a partner. Read *Talk to the Animals Potion* out loud together. Practise the chant in step 4 of the method.

2 Circle the **doing verbs** in *Talk to the Animals Potion.*

3 Write five **doing verbs** of your own that can be found in recipes.

Grammar Rules! Student Book 2 (ISBN 9780655092506) © Tanya Gibb

Alliteration is when sounds are repeated at the beginning of words. *Greedy Godfrey glugged and gurgled 'til it was gone.*
Rhyme is when the ends of words sound the same.

catch *scratch* *patch*

4 Underline the **alliteration** in *Talk to the Animals Potion.*

5 Write the two words that **rhyme** in *Talk to the Animals Potion.*

________________ ________________

6 What do you apply in the Method section of *Talk to the Animals Potion?*

____

7 What is a remedy? Use a dictionary.

____

8 Circle the correct **verb** on each line.

Flamingos [need | needs] their feathers.

Finding an empty snail shell [is | are] difficult.

Using the recipe [is | are] a bad idea.

Marion and Denzel [is | are] good cooks.

Marie [lives | live] in Kellyville.

Tip

Remember the rule about **emotive words** on page 53.

9 Imagine you are going to sell the Talk to the Animals potion. Use paper to create a label for a jar of the potion. Use **emotive words** to persuade people to buy your potion.

If someone uses too much of the Talk to the Animals potion, they need to take a magic remedy. Write a **recipe** for the magic remedy. Use **rhyme** and **alliteration**.

Unit 29

Adjectives, topic sentences, verbs

This text is informative. It is an **information report** about ringtail possums.

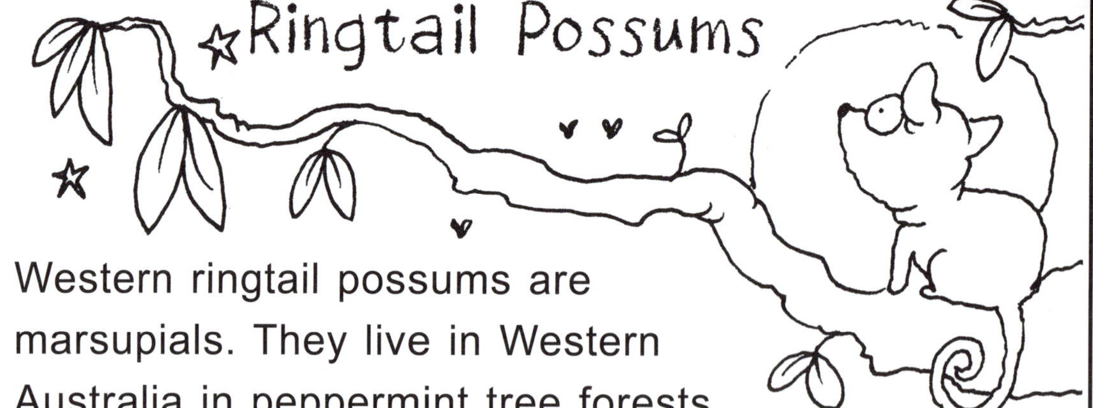

Ringtail Possums

Western ringtail possums are marsupials. They live in Western Australia in peppermint tree forests.

A western ringtail possum has distinctive fur. It is brown with creamy-white fur on its chest and stomach. It has a white tip on its really long tail. It uses its tail to climb trees and carry nesting materials.

Western ringtail possums are active at night. They sleep during the day and live in family groups.

Western ringtails are in danger of extinction. They are dying due to habitat loss. They are also killed by cats, dogs, foxes and cars.

1 Read *Ringtail Possums.* Underline the **noun** *possums.* Circle the **personal pronouns**.

2 Answer each question with an adjective from *Ringtail Possums.*

What colour is the possum's back? ______________

What colour is its chest and stomach? ______________

What colour is the tip of its tail? ______________

How long is its tail? ______________

3 What is habitat loss and how does it happen?

____

____

Grammar Rules! Student Book 2 (ISBN 9780655092506) © Tanya Gibb

4 Write the items in the sequence that uses commas in *Ringtail Possums.*

___

The **topic sentence** of a paragraph is often the first sentence. It tells what the paragraph is about.

5 Write the **topic sentence** of each paragraph in *Ringtail Possums.*

Paragraph 1 ___

Paragraph 2 ___

Paragraph 3 ___

Paragraph 4 ___

6 Write six **prepositional phrases** from *Ringtail Possums.*

___ ___ ___

___ ___ ___

7 Write a **verb** on each line.

Western ringtails ___ in peppermint forests.

The possum ___ white fur on its belly.

The possums ___ during the day.

They ___ active at night.

The possum ___ its tail when climbing.

Find out about an Australian animal. Write a **report**. Write paragraphs telling where it lives, what it looks like and what it does. Make a poster or a brochure to display your information.

Unit 30 Revision

1 Add a **verb** on each line.

Nazeem ______________ a good speller.

Everyone in my family ______________ ice cream.

The recipe ______________ mushrooms.

My dog ______________ hard to train.

Blunt scissors ______________ useless.

Scoobie ______________ Stella's dog.

2 Build vivid descriptions using **adjectives** and **phrases**.

I saw a ______________ possum with ______________.

I saw a ______________ spider with ______________.

I saw a ______________ dog with ______________.

I saw a ______________ cake with ______________.

I saw a ______________ shark with ______________.

3 Circle the **main idea** in the paragraph.

Assistance dogs can help people with physical disabilities by picking up dropped items, opening doors, retrieving the phone, emergency barking and also by just being a companion. Assistance dogs are trained to help people.

Grammar Rules! Student Book 2 (ISBN 9780655092506) © Tanya Gibb

4 Add a **conjunction** to join the sentences. Write the new sentences.

It's too wet to walk to school. Mum will drive us.

___

Tara found a lost dog. She took it home.

___

Sajib is good at maths. He did not finish the test.

___

5 Write **adjectives** that compare on the lines.

Strawberry ice cream tastes good but chocolates tastes ______.

Your cat is pretty but my cat is ______ than yours.

These boots are tough but those boots are the ______ in the shop.

I am tall but my older sister is ______ than me.

6 What is the writer's purpose in each text? Write your answers on the lines.

Buy now! This great deal on soccer balls won't last.

___

Last Saturday, I went to the park with my friends. First we had fun on the equipment. Then we played with a soccer ball. After that we had lunch. ______

Sea lions can move quickly on land and in the water.

___

Biscuit ran as fast as his little legs could carry him and leapt with joy into Lottie's arms. ______

Unit 31

Sentences, pronouns

Corroboree Frogs

This text is informative. It tells where the frogs live, what they look like and about their life cycle.

The southern corroboree frog of Australia is almost extinct. It only lives in a small area of the Snowy Mountains in New South Wales.

Southern corroboree frogs have bright yellow stripes on a black body. The adult frogs are only tiny. They are just over two centimetres long.

Frogs lay eggs. Eggs hatch into tadpoles. The tadpoles of the southern corroboree frog change into frogs when they are one year old. They grow back legs first and then front legs. Then their tails disappear and they become froglets.

1 Read *Corroboree Frogs*. Circle the **personal pronouns**.

2 Draw a cycle diagram on a piece of paper to show how frog eggs become frogs. Label your diagram. Use words and phrases from *Corroboree Frogs*.

3 Use a **being verb** from the box to complete each sentence.

am	is	have	has	are

Frogs ________ amphibians.

Frogs ________ cold blood.

I ________ interested in frogs.

A froglet ________ a tiny tail stump.

A corroboree frog egg ________ like a marble.

Some **pronouns** show possession.

mine ours yours theirs his hers its

Will's handwriting is neater than mine.

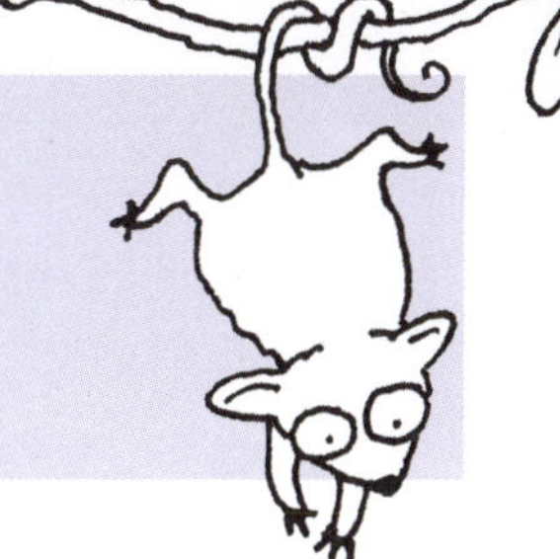

4 Add a **possessive pronoun** to each sentence.

Melissa and Georgia won the diving medal. The medal is ____________.

'I'll give this book to you. It's ____________ from now on,' said Judith.

Sunil said, 'I'll give the game to Olivia. It can be ____________.'

'That hat belongs to me. It's ____________,' declared Manjit.

5 Write the **proper nouns** for where the southern corroboree frogs live.

____

6 Write an extended **noun group** to describe a southern corroboree frog.

____

7 Does the illustration for *Corroboree Frogs* suit the information? Write your opinion and a reason.

____

8 Add commas where necessary.

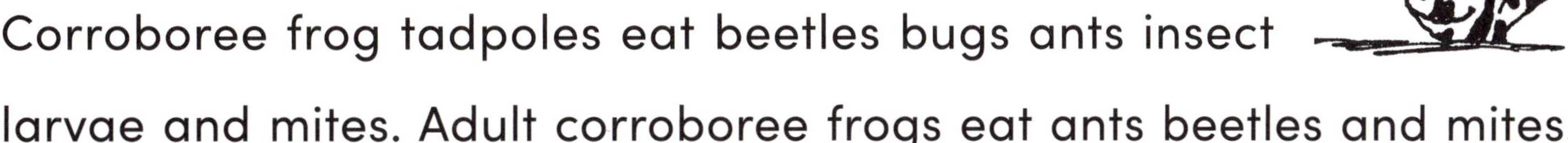

Corroboree frog tadpoles eat beetles bugs ants insect larvae and mites. Adult corroboree frogs eat ants beetles and mites.

Find out about an endangered animal that interests you. Make a class book of **information reports**. Write what the animal looks like, where it lives, what it eats and why it is endangered.

This imaginative text is a **narrative** in the form of a modern-day fable.

The Chimp and the Crocodile

Once upon a time there lived a small chimpanzee. The chimp's name was Charlie.

One day, Charlie was playing on a branch that hung over a lake. Suddenly, the branch snapped. Charlie fell into the lake. Charlie could swim a little bit but not very far. He started to sink into the deep water.

All of a sudden he was lifted to the surface. He took a big gulp of air. A crocodile had saved his life.

The crocodile's name was Winifred. She was a vegetarian. Apples were her favourite food. Charlie decided to collect an enormous basket of apples and other sweet fruit for Winifred every week to thank her.

Charlie and Winifred stayed best friends forever.

1 Read *The Chimp and the Crocodile*. Use words from *The Chimp and the Crocodile* to write what is happening in each drawing.

1. ______________________ ______________________ ______________________	2. ______________________ ______________________ ______________________
3. ______________________ ______________________ ______________________	4. ______________________ ______________________ ______________________

Grammar Rules! Student Book 2 (ISBN 9780655092506) © Tanya Gibb

2 Who is the main character in the story? ______________________

3 Circle the **proper nouns** in *The Chimp and the Crocodile*.

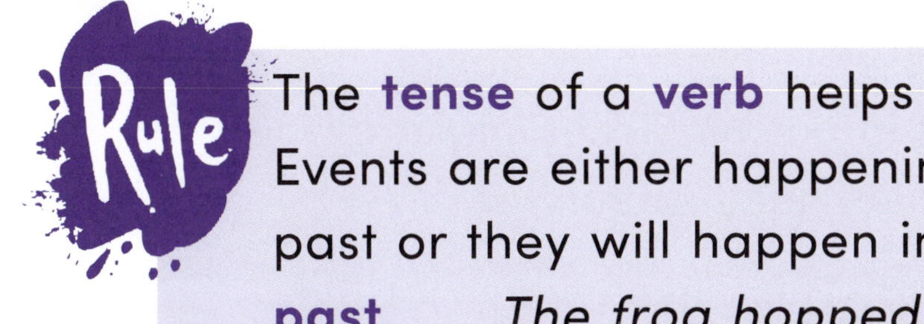

The **tense** of a **verb** helps give a time frame for an event. Events are either happening now, they happened in the past or they will happen in the future.

past *The frog hopped yesterday.*

present *The frog is hopping. A frog hops.*

future *The frog might hop tomorrow.*

4 Complete each sentence. Find **verbs** in *The Chimp and the Crocodile* to tell that events happened in the **past**.

There once ________________ a small chimpanzee.

The chimp was ________________ on a branch.

The branch ________________.

Charlie was ________________ to the surface.

A crocodile had ________________ his life.

Charlie and Winifred ________________ friends forever.

5 Use a **verb** from the box to complete each sentence.

swam
saved
looked
fell

The chimpanzee ________________ into the water.

The crocodile ________________ Charlie.

The crocodile ________________ to the rescue.

The birds in the trees ________________ on.

The Chimp and the Crocodile is a form of **narrative** that is called a fable. Fables have morals. The moral of this fable is 'one good turn deserves another'. Write a fable. Write the moral at the end of your fable.

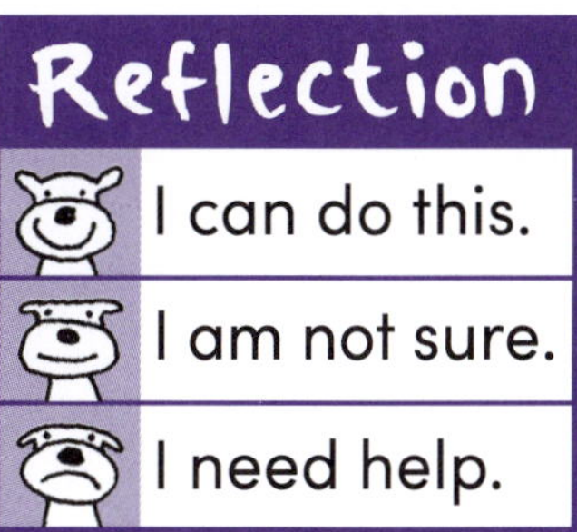

Unit 33

Sentences, proper nouns, verbs

These **instructions** are informative. They tell how to achieve the goal in the title.

How to Help the Environment

- **Plant trees.** Trees provide shelter and food for animals. Trees absorb carbon dioxide, which we don't want in our air. Trees make oxygen, which all animals need to survive.
- **Use less water.** This saves water for the environment. It also saves on energy used to connect water to your home.
- **Recycle everything.** This saves mining or harvesting new materials from the earth and prevents pollution.
- **Use less plastic.** This prevents pollution, saves animals and saves energy.
- **Eat sustainably.** Only buy what you need. Don't waste food. Eat less meat. (Cattle and sheep produce greenhouse gasses, which make climate change worse.)

1 Read *How to Help the Environment*. Circle eight **commands**.

2 What can you do to help the environment in your own home?

____

____

3 What does *They* refer to in paragraph 1? ______________________

4 What does *This* refer to in paragraph 2? ______________________

5 Colour the correct box.

Greenhouse gas is | good | bad |.

Grammar Rules! Student Book 2 (ISBN 9780655092506) © Tanya Gibb

6 Circle the correct **verb** or **verb group** in each sentence.

Cows | creates | create | greenhouse gasses.

Plastic pollution | can hurt | can hurts | animals.

Greenhouse gas | makes | make | climate change worse.

Trees | takes | take | in carbon dioxide.

Plants | releases | release | oxygen to the air.

Rule Names for book titles, organisations or companies are **proper nouns**.

'Belonging' by Jeannie Baker   *Bush Heritage Australia*

Australian Conservation Foundation

7 Rewrite each **sentence** correctly. Check for **proper nouns**.

hayley and flynn joined junior landcare last saturday

____

felix donated money to build predator-proof fences at mount zero-taravale sanctuary to help save bettongs

____

____

lulu read hello and welcome by gregg dreise

____

What should you do if you find an injured animal in your neighbourhood? Find out. Write **instructions** to share in your school or community.

Unit 34

Sentences, conjunctions, verbs

How Sea Animals Breathe

Whales are mammals. They breathe air just like humans. Humans and whales need the oxygen in the air. Whales have one or two nostrils on top of their heads. These nostrils are called blowholes. The whale comes to the surface and blows out all its used air. Used air is air with no oxygen left in it. Then the whale breathes in fresh air. Now it can dive again.

Fish breathe oxygen, too. Their oxygen is dissolved in the water. Fish have sets of flat gills on both sides of their mouths. A fish sucks water into its mouth then pushes the water back out through its gills. As the water flows past the gills, the gills pick up all the oxygen. This is how fish breathe under water.

This text is informative. It **explains** how sea animals breathe.

1 Read *How Sea Animals Breathe*. Draw and label how whales breathe. Draw and label how fish breathe.

Whales	Fish
Breathe out	Breathe in
Breathe in	Breathe out

2 In *How Sea Animals Breathe*, underline three **doing verbs** that whales do.

3 In *How Sea Animals Breathe*, circle three **doing verbs** that fish do.

Grammar Rules! Student Book 2 (ISBN 9780655092506) © Tanya Gibb

4 Draw lines to join the parts of the **sentences**. Hint! The underlined words will help you join correctly.

Because whales are mammals,	then it breathes in fresh air.
Humans are mammals	but they don't breathe air.
The whale breathes out used air	they need to breathe air.
Fish need oxygen	so they need to breathe air.
Whales need to surface	otherwise they will die.
Animals need oxygen	so they can breathe.

5 Use **nouns** from *How Sea Animals Breathe* to complete the sentences.

Whales and fish breathe ______________ but they breathe differently.

Whales breathe through their ______________.

Whales breathe at the ______________ of the water.

Fish breathe through their ______________.

Fish breathe under ______________.

6 Join the simple sentences. Rewrite the new sentences.

My soup had gone cold. I heated it in the microwave.

____

Theo returned the shirt to the shop. He noticed it had a stain.

____

Find out how humans breathe. How do we get oxygen out of the air? Write an **explanation**. Or, draw a series of diagrams to explain how we breathe. Label your diagrams.

Unit 35 Revision

1 Circle the **noun groups** and **pronouns** that refer to the hermit crab.

I couldn't find my hermit crab. It had escaped from its tank. I looked in my bedroom. I looked in the kitchen and in the bathroom. I looked in the lounge room. I found it in the laundry. It was hiding under a wet mop.

2 Underline the **prepositional phrases** that tell where.

I couldn't find my hermit crab. It had escaped from its tank. I looked in my bedroom. I looked in the kitchen and in the bathroom. I looked in the lounge room. I found it in the laundry. It was hiding under a wet mop.

3 Add a **verb** of your own to each sentence.

Hermit crabs ______________ shells.

A corroboree frog ______________ yellow stripes.

I ______________ interested in spiders.

Ariana ______________ to swim.

Samesh always ______________ to the baby.

4 Rewrite each sentence with correct punctuation.

tim told sasha that zoos victoria is helping frogs

____

the zoo is trying to save frogs bandicoots skinks and possums

____

5 Write a **proper noun** to name a baby dinosaur. ______________________

Grammar Rules! Student Book 2 (ISBN 9780655092506) ©Tanya Gibb

6 Circle the correct **verb** to show the action was in the past.

I played | play recorder in the concert last night.

Dad work | worked all yesterday, painting the fence.

Mum is mowing | mowed the lawn this morning.

I help | helped Katrina earlier.

My sister make | made mud pies after breakfast.

7 Circle the **verb** in each **sentence**. Tick the sentences that are **commands**.

Hermit crabs swap shells.

Buy extra shells for the tank.

Touch your hermit crabs gently.

Hermit crabs run quickly.

Clean your hermit crab tank.

8 Unscramble and rewrite the **sentences** correctly.

chickens from hatch eggs ______________________________

go aunty sia with I'll ______________________________

for the spider out watch ______________________________

the magpies nesting are ______________________________

9 Draw lines to join the **clauses** correctly. Hint! The underlined words wlll help you join correctly.

<u>Because</u> we need milk,	<u>then</u> I'll pack the picnic basket.
We'll take the dog too,	<u>but</u> we probably won't need them.
I'll make sandwiches	I'll walk to the shop.
We'll take raincoats	<u>so</u> we can sit on the ground.
We'll take a blanket	<u>otherwise</u> she'll be upset.

Glossary

Look at the page number in the circle to find more information about the rule or tip.

adjective............a word that tells you more about a **noun** 21

comparing adjective 57

point out in a noun group 58

quantity/number adjective 41

show ownership in a noun group 58

adverb...............a word or phrase that can tell where, 27 when 27 or how 39

alliteration..........when sounds are repeated at the beginning of words 63

antonym..............a word that means the opposite to another word 23

article.................a small word (*a, an, the*) used in front of a **noun** or at the start of a **noun group** 41

clause..................a group of words that includes a **verb**

a main clause (independent clause) is a complete message 24

a simple sentence is one clause 11 14

subject of a clause 14

comma.................a punctuation mark that separates parts of a sentence or words in a series 12

command.............a sentence that tells someone to do something 32

compound sentence.............a sentence consisting of two **main clauses** joined by a **coordinating conjunction** 24

compound word..a word formed by combining two other words 35

conjunction..........a word that connects words, phrases or **clauses** 24

coordinating conjunction 24

emotive word......a word that appeals to the emotions 53

exclamation.........a sentence that shows strong emotion, or gives a warning or command 28

main idea............the idea the writer or speaker wants you to believe or accept 36

noun....................a word for a person, place, animal or thing

common and proper 9

extended noun groups 61

noun group 41

singular and plural 38

onomatopoeia.....the name given to words that sound like the things they represent 29

paragraph............a sentence or a number of sentences based on the same idea 56

topic sentence 65

personal pronoun.................a word that is used in place of a **noun** 33

possessive pronoun.................a pronoun that shows possession or ownership 69

prepositional phrase ....a group of words beginning with a preposition and including a **noun** or **pronoun**; can tell where, when or how 27

question.................a **sentence** that asks for information or an opinion 46

quoted speech.....the actual speech someone said; uses quotation marks 17

rhyme......................when the ends of words sound the same 63

sentence................a group of words that makes sense on its own. It must include at least one **verb.** 11

compound 24

simple 11

statement of fact or opinion 46

sequence ....the way events and ideas in a text are ordered in time (chronologically) or casually 25

statement ....a **sentence** that gives a fact or an opinion 46

synonym ....a word that has a similar meaning to another word 37

time connective....a connecting word that helps sequence events in time 25

verb..........................a word or group of words that tells what is happening in a **clause**

being (relating) 11

doing 9

saying 16

tense 71

thinking 22